"Teach me your way, Lord and lead me in a plain path."

Psalm 27:11

Instructions for life from the red letters.

The Jesus Handbook

Teresa L. Hoffman

The Jesus Handbook, Instructions for Life from the Red Letters

2nd Edition: January 2022

By Teresa L. Hoffman

ISBN: 978-1-716-61788-1

Cover Art by Anointing Productions.

Published by Teresa Hoffman/ Lulu Press, Inc.

Holy Ground Life Ministries: PO Box 432, Fawnskin, CA 92333

Visit our website: holygroundlife.com

Available for individual purchase: Lulu.com/spotlight/holygroundlife

and Amazon Kindle eBook.

†

To Joshua and Micah Rose. You can do all things through Jesus. He will always be your strength.
I love you.

A very special thank you to:

Tom and Mary, my mother and father, now citizens of Heaven. Thank you for believing this book should be published.

Shawn, my beloved husband, for your endless encouragement. You are my "faith" hero.

To the many men and women of God who have taught me the uncompromising Word of God, especially Pastors John & Michele Dunn, Pastors Mel & Desiree Ayres, and Kenneth & Gloria Copeland.

And finally, thank you to my faith-filled, "Word Warriors":
Michele, Diana, Tabitha, and Suzan.
As iron sharpens iron, so a friend sharpens a friend.
Proverbs 27:17 NLT

"Who do you say that I am?" - *Jesus Christ of Nazareth*

Jesus.

He was born 2,224 years ago. Every major world religion gives an opinion of Him. His name is placed in history books among the most influential humans to ever walk the earth. Approximately 2.3 billion men and women, at this moment, call themselves followers of Jesus. Traditions have been created. Churches have been built. Denominations have risen up. The teachings of this one man, Jesus, have been passed down through many generations. But like a spiritual game of "telephone," Jesus' words have often become distorted. Sadly, He is one of the most misunderstood and misquoted people in history.

Who do you say He is?

The only way to truly know someone is to hear from them directly.

Jesus is calling you to come close. He wants to speak to you, simply, without the bindings of religiosity. He is the living expression of the Word of God. He is the same Jesus who sat in humble homes with men and women sharing the love of God while holding the little ones on His lap. He is reaching out His hand in friendship to reveal Himself to you. A gentle man, with the authority of the One who made the universe, calls you to follow Him.

His perfect love draws you in and captures you. It holds you and calls you important. It heals you and leaves no doubt you are safe in it. It is a love that stood up in your place when all of Hell condemned you. He went to unimaginable places of torment, so you wouldn't have to. Once He took the power of death from harming you, He opened the door to Heaven for you.

In light of this unconditional love, we cannot help but love Jesus with our whole heart in return.

But how do we love Him?

He said in John 14:15, “If you really love Me, then keep my commandments.”

What are His commandments?

In my search for them, I went directly to the source. I found them in the red letters of the Bible: Jesus’ own words. In this book, you will find every commandment spoken by Jesus during His earthly ministry. I did not want to use any other religious books or traditions, but only the carefully recorded words of Jesus Himself found in the four gospels.

His words in red have brought life, light, freedom, truth, and wisdom to every generation since His feet walked this earth. His commandments are as relevant today as they were when He first spoke them. They are life to us. They are the key to living an overcoming life filled with hope and joy.

Jesus’ commandments not only navigate us to abundant life, they navigate us to the place of overwhelming love...to God Himself. His commandments connect us intimately to the Father.

When we honor these commandments, we become separated from the darkness of this world. We enter His Kingdom on earth and in it we have peace to withstand any storm, healing to repair anything that is broken, wisdom to light up any circumstance, strength for any weakness, and forgiveness without limit.

Our obedience to His commandments, ushers in a wave of blessing.

The commandments of Jesus are listed here for you to clearly follow. Carve out a section of time each day to focus and meditate on what Jesus is saying to you. I encourage you to write down what He is speaking to you personally as you hear His voice through the red letters.

Have the Bible on hand to reference all the scriptures that point to that particular commandment. The Word of God is "alive and active" and it will fill you with wisdom, understanding, and direction. When Jesus repeats a commandment in several scriptures, pay close attention, these are the key commandments He wants you to hear.

If you read a commandment and feel condemnation for not following it, remember, "Not a single person on earth is always good and never sins" (Ecclesiastes 7:20). None of us are perfect, but we are called to perfection. Smith Wigglesworth said, "If you miss the mark of holiness ten times a day, fortify yourself to believe that God intends for you to be holy, and then stand again." Remember, Jesus paid the price for your sin and condemnation has no place in your life. You are the righteousness of God in Christ Jesus your Savior.

In a broken world that has shifting foundations we look to Jesus Christ, our Rock, to guide us in all things and navigate the narrow path that leads to eternal life.

I pray a blessing over you as you hear from the One who passionately wants you have an abundant life.

In Him,

Teresa Hoffman

†

"For if you tell others with your own mouth
that Jesus Christ is your Lord
and believe in your own heart that God has raised Him from the dead,
you will be saved.
For it is by believing in his heart that a person becomes right with God;
and with his mouth he tells others of his faith,
confirming his salvation."
Romans 10:9-10

Prayer

Father God, I believe in Jesus Christ, your Son, as my Savior.
I believe He was sent by You.
I believe He died on the cross for my sins, and I believe He rose from the dead. When He rose, He stripped death of its power over me.
I believe He now sits with you until He comes again in glory on this earth.
I repent of my sin and receive your forgiveness.
I receive your gift of the Holy Spirit to guide me and strengthen me.
I receive Your rest.
Come into my heart, Jesus, and live there as Lord over my life.
I want to follow You today.

Contents

Whoever has my commandments and knows them is the one who loves me. The one who loves me will be loved by my Father, and I too will love them, and show myself to them.

John 14:21

Commandments of Jesus

Follow Me.

Red Letters

Jesus said to them, "Follow Me [as My disciples, accepting Me as your Master and Teacher and walking the same path of life that I walk], and I will make you fishers of men." Matthew 4:19 AMP

This is the commandment Jesus repeated the most during His ministry here on earth. We are to follow Him in everything.

How do you follow someone? You watch them closely.
How did Jesus treat others? How did He deal with the enemy of God? How did He pray? How did He love? How did He obey His Father's commands?

The world will loudly point you in its direction if you are not listening to your Savior. Following the world's system will always lead you into darkness. As you go on in the world's way, your life will become more and more self-sustaining. This self-obsession will cause you anxiety and frustration. Provision, justice, safety and salvation will be in *your* hands instead of God's hands. And your hands won't be enough.

In His gentle voice, Jesus says, "Follow Me." Leave the need for constant control and let Him lead. As you do, He will give you wisdom for every circumstance and peace that the world cannot provide. Living light will flood your path.

As you read on, you will find commandments that begin with "*Follow Me in this*". Jesus' actions and choices when He walked the earth are commandments for us to follow Him in the same way.

Remember this: You do not need to be perfect to follow Jesus. You need to be willing to continue to follow Him, even if you fall.

Prayer

"Lord, today I choose to hear Your voice first. I choose to follow You. I will resist looking to the waves of this world and I look to You."

Jesus' Words that Point to this Commandment

Matthew 4:19-20, Matthew 8:22, Matthew 9:9, Matthew 10:38-39, Matthew 16:24-25, Matthew 19:21, Matthew 19:28-29, Mark 1:17-18, Mark 2:14, Mark 8:34-35, Mark 10:21, Luke 5:27-28, Luke 6:39-40, Luke 9:23-25, Luke 9:59-62, Luke 14:27, Luke 17:33, Luke 18:22, John 1:43, John 8:12, John 10:27-29, John 12:26, John 13:36, John 21:19-22

> *Jesus said to the people, "I am the Light of the world. So, if you follow me, you won't be stumbling through the darkness, for living light will flood your path."*
>
> *John 8:12 TLB*

How can I apply this to my life?

___

___

___

___

___

___

___

___

___

Love God with Everything You Call Your Own and Love People.

Red Letters

> *Jesus said, "The most important of all the commandments is this: 'The Lord Yahweh, our God is one!' You are to love the Lord Yahweh your God, with every passion of your heart, with all the energy of your being, with every thought that is within you, and with all your strength. This is the great and supreme commandment. And the second is this: You must love your neighbor in the same way you love yourself. You will never find a greater commandment than these. Mark 12:29-30 TPT*

The most important commandment Jesus gave you is to love. This love He asks you to release to others comes from the love that was first poured into you. God's love was poured into your heart through the Holy Spirit who was given to you by Jesus. (Romans 5:5). Remember this, God loves *you* with all the passion of *His* heart, Jesus loved *you* with all the strength of *His* being when He went to the cross for you, and the Holy Spirit loves *you* continuously with every thought He has toward you (His thoughts touch your thought, comforting you and reminding you of the promises of Jesus Christ, your Savior).

This love sets you apart from the world (John 13:35). It is an intense love that changes atmospheres.

Instead of holding tightly to what is yours in fear, you can release anything with this love. You can lay open what is vulnerable through the power of this love. You can trust God even when circumstances are shaken. You can love your neighbor even if it seems impossible. You grow up in this love instead of shrinking into the dark void of self-centeredness.

This God-kind of love produces patience, kindness, integrity, gentleness, an easy yielding to joy, a peace-seeking attitude, and an everlasting mindset toward life. When we yield to this love, it produces believers who are faithful, selfless, fearless, sacrificial, unconditionally-loving, giving, courageous, self-controlled, passionate, trusting, edifying, always thinking the best, truth seeking, never quitting, believing, and strong. More than ever, this soul-sick world needs believers to demonstrate the love of God.

When you release your love towards God, He builds that love-fire in you. When the love of God burns within you, the world gets set on fire with His love. This is why it is Jesus' first and most important commandment.

Prayer

"Father, I love you. I give you all that I am. Take my life. Let Your love-fire burn brightly within me. Burn out everything that is not of You. I receive Your love for me and let it flow toward others."

Jesus' Words that Point to this Commandment

Matthew 22:37-40, Mark 12:29-34, Luke 10:25-28

> *Jesus said, "Love the Lord your God with all your passion and prayer and intelligence. This is the most important, the first on any list. But there is a second to set alongside it: Love others as well as you love yourself. These two commands are pegs; everything in God's Law and the Prophets hangs from them." Matthew 22:39 MSG*

How can I apply this to my life?

____

____

____

Receive Me as the Messiah.

Red Letters

The woman said, "Well, at least I know that the Messiah will come—the one they call Christ—and when he does, he will explain everything to us." Then Jesus told her, "I am the Messiah!" John 4:25-26 TLB

So many religions acknowledge Jesus. They call Him a prophet, a good teacher, an important religious figure, a miracle worker, a god, an enlightened man and a holy man. Jesus very clearly declared, "I am the Messiah. I am the Christ, the Anointed One."

Messiah means "a king who is sent by God to *deliver* His people from evil." Christ means "the Anointed One." God anointed Jesus with the "burden-removing power of God" (Isaiah 10:27) for you.

Receiving Jesus as Messiah means acknowledging you need a deliverer. The burden of sin was placed on you the moment Adam disobeyed and there is no amount of good that can remove that burden. There is no earthly cleansing that you could go through that would make you pure in the sight of God. Sin locked you in an automatic prison. But God...in His amazing love for you, sent His only son from heaven to earth to deliver you and set you free.

Jesus became the eternal sacrifice that paid the price to destroy your burden forever. He not only set you free, because of Him, you are made pure in the sight of God without the blemish of sin.
Jesus is the only One who delivers you from the power of sin and its destruction. Your Messiah and His anointing removes your burdens and destroys the enemy's oppressive plan over you.

Every prophecy in the Old Testament regarding the Messiah, Jesus fulfilled. He is the long-awaited Messiah. If you have never accepted this, now is the time. Jesus is God's gift of deliverance presented to you.

If this seems too good to be true, I invite you to experience the overwhelming goodness of God. It is not your perfection He desires. He is simply asking you to receive the greatest gift ever given, Jesus Christ.

Prayer

"Jesus, I believe you are my Messiah. You live in me. Thank you for taking all the burdens and breaking all the chains that held me down. I will not take them up again."

Jesus' Words that Point to this Commandment

Matthew 16:15-19, Mark 8:29, Luke 7:18-23, Luke 9:20, John 3:12-15, John 4:25-26, John 14:6, John 20:28-29

> *The disciples of John the Baptist soon heard of all that Jesus was doing. When they told John about it, he sent two of his disciples to Jesus to ask him, "Are you really the Messiah? Or shall we keep on looking for him?" (Jesus responded) "Go back to John and tell him all you have seen and heard here today: how those who were blind can see. The lame are walking without a limp. The lepers are completely healed. The deaf can hear again. The dead come back to life. And the poor are hearing the Good News. And tell him,*
> *Blessed is the one who does not lose his faith in me."*
> *Luke 7:18-23 TLB*
> *(These were all Hebrew descriptions of the Messianic reign.)*

How can I apply this to my life?

____

____

____

____

____

Do Not Worry.

Red Letters

Jesus said, "Do not let your heart be troubled. Believe in God...believe in Me." John 14:1 NKJV

Worry is having faith in a negative outcome.

Your mind is a powerful gift. It can be used to formulate groundbreaking visions or unseen terrors. Grab the reins and direct it. The best way to direct it is with your mouth. Thoughts rarely overcome other thoughts, but the words you speak will direct your thoughts. Steer your faith toward His abundant life by speaking to anxiety with the Word of God.

When a storm of worry begins, start by saying, "Stop! God has not given me a spirit of fear but of power, love and a sound mind (2 Timothy 1:7). I *will* trust God and this situation will turn around for good and glorify God!" (Romans 8:28).

Find His promises regarding your situation and continually speak to that mountain of fear until it dissolves like grains of sand into the ocean. Don't let anxiety take up any space in your mind.

There is one thing you can be absolutely assured of now and in the future, God reigns. You have a Father in Heaven that cares for you with a personal love. You have a Savior who knows what the pressures of life feel like and He is daily speaking to your heart, "This is the way."

As the sun rises, so does a new day with new possibilities.
Don't waste your thoughts on what bad news might come. God's plans for you are good.

Be filled with hope as you trust in Him.

Prayer

"Lord, I will not be afraid. You are not worried, so I choose not to be either. I will trust in You. Your plans for me are very good and nothing can separate me from Your love."

Jesus' Words that Point to this Commandment

Matthew 6:25-34, Matthew 11:28-30, Matthew 28: 18-20, Mark 4:18-20,

Luke 12:22-34, John 14:1-4, John 14:27

> *Jesus said, "So, don't be anxious about tomorrow. God will take care of your tomorrow too. Live one day at a time."*
> *Matthew 6:34 TLB*

How can I apply this to my life?

____

____

____

____

____

____

____

While he was still speaking, behold, a bright cloud overshadowed them, and a voice from the cloud said, "This is My beloved Son, with whom I am well-pleased and delighted! Listen to Him!"

Matthew 17:5 AMP

Study Who I Am.

Red Letters

Jesus prayed, "And this is the way to have eternal life—by knowing you, the only true God, and Jesus Christ, the one you sent to earth!"

John 17:3 TLB

Don't take someone else's word for it. Study who Jesus is.

"Learn of Me," He says, "For I am gentle and humble in heart, and you will find rest for your souls" (Matthew 11:29 NIV). The more you learn about your Savior, the more your faith will grow and the more you will rest in Him.

Trust is formed when you make a commitment to someone after observing trustworthy behavior. The only way to know if someone is trustworthy is to study them and spend time with them. You do not gain trust through someone else's opinion.

Read the scriptures to hear His voice. Seek Him in prayer and spend time in His presence. Get so close to Him and His ways that you can hear His heartbeat and what moves Him. This is the absolute key to walking the Christian life.

Don't be satisfied with what your teachers have told you about Jesus. Don't be satisfied with Christian social media phrases or your parent's faith. Purpose to seek who He is in the Old Testament and the New.

You will discover the depth of His love toward you. It might be overwhelming because in reality, He has studied you. He knows your coming and going. He knows your heartbeat. He knows your weaknesses and strengths, your struggles and triumphs. And you are intimately loved.

When he first met Jesus, Nathanael said, "How do you know anything about me?" Jesus said to Nathanael, "I saw you under the fig tree." Nathanael was shocked because he was all alone there! He had not met Jesus. Because of this he declared Jesus must be the Messiah.

Jesus then told him, "From now on you will see an open Heaven and gaze upon the Son of Man- *the messianic term for Christ"* (John 1:48-51). Jesus was going to be known by Nathanael.

Make it your decision to study the One who is the Lover of your soul, your Creator, your Deliverer and your Savior. His heart is towards you.

Prayer

"Lord, I want to know You. I want to know what moves You. I want to know who I am in You."

Jesus' Words that Point to this Commandment

Matthew 11:29, John 1:1-5,9-18, John 7:28-29, John 8:10-12, John 8:58, John 10:9-18, 27-30, John 14:6-7, John 15:15, John 17:3

> *Jesus told him, "I am the Way—yes, and the Truth and the Life. No one can get to the Father except by means of me. If you had known who I am, then you would have known who my Father is. From now on you know him—and have seen him!"*
>
> *John 14:6-7 TLB*

How can I apply this to my life?

____

____

____

____

Make a Definitive Choice.

Red Letters

Jesus said, "I am the Door; anyone who enters in through Me will be saved (will live).
John 10:9 AMP

Picture a holy place with many windows but only one red door.
People are gathered looking in the windows and desiring to enter. There are flags and bells, loud voices, and every kind of distraction and type of entertainment surrounding this holy place. But inside is the glow of perfect peace.

Jesus stands quietly at the red door and calls your name. He says, "I am the door leading to everlasting life. I paid the sacrifice for you to enter. Come in, my friend."

In dark corners, there are false entrances that claim to give entrance but only lead to empty spaces. Some say, "Don't be a fool, all of these doors enter the Holy Place." Some doors are titled, "For only those who are good enough."

Jesus looks you in the eye and says, "If anyone else comes to you and says they can lead you in, apart from Me, they are a thief. Do not follow them."

Jesus will call you with His unconditional love, but you will make the choice to enter. Don't wander in circles. Don't be deceived. Don't wait.

When you walk through, you will be passing through His sacrifice on the cross. Every sin will be absorbed. Earthly garments will be replaced with white ones threaded with His righteousness. This is not religion, this is transformation by relationship with the Son of God.

If you walked in without His sacrifice, your sin would be destroyed in the holy place and you with it. Walk through His door and never turn back.

Prayer

"Lord Jesus, thank you. You have unlocked the door of eternal life for me. I have made my decision and want to enter and sit down with You. I never want to leave. I am home with You."

Jesus' Words that Point to this Commandment

Matthew 25:1-13, Luke 11:9-10, Luke 13:24-29, John 10:1-11, John 14:6

> *Jesus said, "But while they were gone, the bridegroom came, and those who were ready went in with him to the marriage feast, and the door was locked." Matthew 25:10 TLB*

How can I apply this to my life?

____

____

____

____

____

____

God, teach me lessons for living, so I can stay the course. Give me insight, so I can do what you tell me– my whole life one long, obedient response. Guide me down the road of your commandments; I love traveling this freeway! Psalm 119:33-35 MSG

Be Born of the Spirit.

Red Letters

Jesus said, "For God loved the world so much that he gave his only Son so that anyone who believes in him shall not perish but have eternal life."
John 3:16 TLB

Everyone who is alive in this kingdom called Earth was born out of water from their mother. God's hand personally shaped you from the beginning within your mother(Psalm 139:13), and the breath you breathe was given by Him (Genesis 2:7). He gave you life. A life that now has a beginning and an end.

Jesus, the Son of God, came to call you and I to be born *again* out of the Spirit of the Living God and have eternal life.

When you are born again your inner man (the spirit) is woven together with the same substance that makes up the Almighty Living God. Your spiritual DNA is transformed. When this happens, you are able to enter into the Kingdom of Heaven here on earth and have entrance, when your earthly life is over, into the Kingdom of God.

How do you get born of the Spirit? Believe in God's gift, Jesus.

It is your choice to enter into relationship with God as His child.
There is no price to pay. Jesus paid it. There is no work to be done. Jesus did it.

This simple act of faith will be the most profound decision you will ever make. The playing field is level, and all are invited.

When you make this decision, you are "delivered" through the cross into new life. You begin to breathe by the spirit. You begin to see by the spirit. You begin to hear by the spirit.

Jesus says, "I speak an eternal truth: Unless you are born of water and Spirit-Wind you will never enter God's kingdom realm. For the natural realm can only give birth to things that are natural, but the spiritual realm gives birth to supernatural life!" (John 3:5-6 TPT).

Prayer

"Jesus, I believe. I receive this concept by faith. My spirit is born of You. Help me to renew my mind to Your way of thinking. Help me unlock all the treasure you have for me in Your Word."

Jesus' Words that Point to this Commandment

John 1:10-13, John 3:3-8, John 3:16, John 4:24, John 6:44-47

> *Jesus replied, "With all the earnestness I possess I tell you this: Unless you are born again, you can never get into the Kingdom of God.*
> *John 3:3 TLB*

How can I apply this to my life?

____

____

____

____

____

I delight to fulfill Your will, my God, for Your living words are written upon the pages of my heart.

Psalm 40:8 TPT

Pursue the Kingdom of God.

Red Letters

Jesus said, "But seek first the Kingdom of God, and His righteousness; and all these things shall be added unto you."
Matthew 6:33 KJV

If you decided to travel to a special place here on earth, you would first get directions. Then you would make plans on how to get there: transportation, accommodations, and maybe an itinerary. Pursuing this destination would require your time, money, and research.

Jesus commands us to seek out the Kingdom of God. But this kingdom is not a location here on earth. His kingdom is found in the hearts of His children. Its location is in another dimension.

You pursue this kingdom in the same way you would a physical kingdom. You research Jesus: the perfect reflection of God. He is your transportation and your entrance point. You become fueled with the promises of His Word regarding who you are and who He is. You make daily plans to rest in Him. You learn the language of faith and begin to speak it.

As your understanding grows, the Kingdom grows within you. The currency is trust. You spend time learning how to apply this truth to everything: *Trust in the Lord always and don't lean on your own reasoning (Proverbs 3:5).*

This is a kingdom that, once you arrive, you never wish to leave. The environment is one of peace and blessings. It is where true freedom reigns. But your pursuit must continue daily as you move deeper into His Kingdom.

Your number one priority should be to learn how the Kingdom of God operates and how you operate in it, here on earth. You are already on your way. The roadmap for that journey is found in the commandments of Jesus.

This is "the way" to everything you need. Jesus said, "I am the way, the truth and the life. The only way to the Father is through me." John 14:6

Prayer

"Lord, when I wake, I seek You. Guide me in the way I should go. I study Your living Word and let it move me and move my circumstances. My eyes and ears are open to new revelations as I spend time with You. I pursue You."

Jesus' Words that Point to this Commandment

Matthew 4:17, Matthew 6:33, Matthew 13:11-23, Matthew 19:13-24, Mark 1:15-17, Mark 4:26-32, Mark 9:35-37, Luke 17:20-21, Luke 12:28-32, John 3:3-8, John 18:36-37

Jesus said, "The Kingdom of God does not come with observation: Nor will they say, 'See here!' or, 'See there!' for, indeed, the Kingdom of God is within you." Luke 17:20-21 NKJV

How can I apply this to my life?

____

____

____

____

____

____

Don't Let Your Religion Serve You, Serve Others with Your Christianity.

Red Letters

Follow Me in this:

Jesus replied, "Is there a person here who, finding one of your lambs fallen into a ravine, wouldn't, even though it was a Sabbath, pull it out? Surely kindness to people is as legal as kindness to animals!" Then he said to the man, "Hold out your hand." He held it out and it was healed. The Pharisees walked out furious, sputtering about how they were going to ruin Jesus." Matthew 12:12 (MSG)

Religion will draw you into laws and rules and away from loving people. Remember to love people first.

Take care of people. Have mercy on them. Jesus made it clear that he wants you to focus on "mercy" not sacrifice. He wants you to follow Him and urge sinners to God. He is not interested in self-righteous men and women (Matthew 9:13).

It was the religious, when Jesus walked the earth, that missed the promised Messiah. They were so tangled in their laws they couldn't see Him. Do not miss what the Lord wants for you because you are trying to impress Him with your "Christianity" and hurting others in the process.

Mercy embraces. Mercy seeks healing, not punishment. Mercy does not judge. Mercy offers space, not pressure. Mercy is a beautiful response to what is ugly.

Over and over God has shown His children tender love and mercy.

Reflect the love of God toward people and you will wear the garment of pure dedication in the sight of God.

Prayer

"Lord, wash me clean of trying to be perfect. Your righteousness is all I need. Help me see people the way You see them. Help me love them the way You do."

Jesus' Words that Point to this Commandment

Matthew 12:1-13, Matthew 25:41-46, Mark 2:27- 28, Mark 3: 4-8, Luke 6:1-11, Luke 6:9, Luke 10:30-37, Luke 11:37-52, Luke 13:13-17, Luke 14:3-14, Luke 22:25-26, John 5:7-18, John 7:22-24, John 9:14-16, John 13:4-7

> *Then Jesus addressed them, "Let me ask you something: What kind of action suits the Sabbath best? Doing good or doing evil? Helping people or leaving them helpless?"*
>
> *Luke 6:9 MSG*

How can I apply this to my life?

____

____

____

____

____

The one who keeps God's word is the person in whom we see God's mature love. This is the only way to be sure we're in God. Anyone who claims to be intimate with God ought to live the same kind of life Jesus lived. 1 John 2:4-6 MSG

Never Lie. Put All Deceit Away from You.

Red Letters

Jesus said, "Why can't you understand what I am saying? It is because you are prevented from doing so! For you are the children of your father the devil and you love to do the evil things he does. He was a murderer from the beginning and a hater of truth—there is not an iota of truth in him.

When he lies, it is perfectly normal; for he is the father of liars."

John 8:43-44 TLB

When you lie you separate yourself from God, because He is Truth. This dark road of separation twists itself into more lies and eventually leads to destruction... every time.

Make a choice right now to be truthful in everything. You will discover the freedom it will produce.

Lies always begin with fear. Fear puts you in bondage and in a small space of thinking.
Truth brings you to a wide-open space. It also brings health to your mind.

The apostle Peter writes this to you, "Friends, you have been chosen and destined by Father God. The Holy Spirit has set you apart to be God's holy ones, obedient followers of Jesus Christ (1 Peter 1:2) and Jesus 'Never sinned and He never spoke deceitfully' (1 Peter 2:22 quoting Isaiah 53:9) so whoever wants to embrace true life and find beauty in each day must stop speaking evil, hurtful words and never deceive in what they say (1 Peter 3:11)."

Small lies. Big lies. They are all the same. God hates lying (Proverbs 6:16-19).

Prayer

"Lord, forgive me for lying. Help me break any patterns of deceit. I speak the truth in love today."

Jesus' Words that Point to this Commandment

Matthew 15:16-20, Matthew 19:18-19, Mark 10:19, Luke 16:10, Luke 18:20, John 3:19-21, John 8:31-47

Jesus said, "But those who love the truth will come out into the Light and welcome its exposure, for the Light will reveal that their fruitful works were produced by God."

John 3:21 TPT

How can I apply this to my life?

____

____

____

____

____

____

____

____

____

See if there is any path of pain I'm walking on, and lead me back to your glorious, everlasting way-the path that brings me back to You.

Psalm 139:24 TPT

Love Others as You Love Yourself.

Red Letters

Jesus said, "You must love your neighbor in the same way you love yourself."

Mark 12:31

How do you love yourself?
You feed, clothe, comfort, protect, celebrate, give attention to, and extend grace to yourself for bad reactions. Now do these to your fellow man.

Take time to feed, clothe, and comfort others. Protect those who are weak. Celebrate and give attention to those who are forgotten. Extend the same grace and excuses you give yourself to the one who tries your patience.

Why? Because Jesus first loved us, and this love is what birthed us into believers. It is by this love we have eternal life. It is His love that feeds our spirit-man. To everyone we meet, we should be known by this love.

Remind yourself the part of you that has difficulty loving others is the part that died with Christ. You were born again into His love.

All of the law and every commandment flows through two great commandments. This is one of them. It is a super commandment. The first is to love Father God with all you call your own, and the second is to love your neighbor as you love yourself. If commandments were doors, these would be the first double doors that give entrance to all the others.

Jesus said, "So this is MY command: Love each other deeply, as much as I have loved you. For the greatest love of all is a love that sacrifices all.

And this great love is demonstrated when a person sacrifices his life for his friends" (John 15:12 TPT).

Prayer

"Lord, thank you for pouring your love into me every hour. Your love never fails. Your love covers a multitude of sins. Help me walk in this love today."

Jesus' Words that Point to this Commandment

Matthew 19:19, Matthew 22:36-40, Mark 12:28-34, Mark 6:34-44, Luke 10:25-37, John 15:12-13, John 21:15-17

> *Jesus replied with an illustration: "A Jew going on a trip from Jerusalem to Jericho was attacked by bandits. They stripped him of his clothes and money and beat him up and left him lying half dead beside the road. By chance a Jewish priest came along; and when he saw the man lying there, he crossed to the other side of the road and passed him by. A Jewish Temple-assistant walked over and looked at him lying there, but then went on. But a despised Samaritan came along, and when he saw him, he felt deep pity. Kneeling beside him the Samaritan soothed his wounds with medicine and bandaged them. Then he put the man on his donkey and walked along beside him till they came to an inn, where he nursed him through the night. The next day he handed the innkeeper two twenty-dollar bills and told him to take care of the man. 'If his bill runs higher than that,' he said, 'I'll pay the difference the next time I am here.' Now which of these three would you say was a neighbor to the bandits' victim?"*
>
> *The man replied, "The one who showed him some pity." Then Jesus said, "Yes, now go and do the same." Luke 10:30-37 TLB*

How can I apply this to my life?

____

____

Receive My Peace.

Red Letters

Jesus said, "Peace be unto you...Peace be unto you...Peace be unto you."
John 20:19,21,26

Remember, this is a command, not just something to console you.

The peace Jesus is asking you to freely receive is not a worldly peace where your environment is quiet and tranquil. It is a supernatural gift and it is received by faith not by feelings. It is a heavenly peace that is given to you and it seals you eternally.

Your faith will need to grasp it. When you do, it will secure your heart even when the storms of life rage around you. Waves of fear may be crashing against you, but this peace anchors your soul.

It is a gift that speaks to you and reminds you of what God has promised you. It is a gift that you must guard. Be diligent to not let anxiety or fear take its place.

When bad circumstances threaten you, fear will try to make a wedge to separate you from that peace.
You must immediately react with a firm decision to not let go of His promise.

If the storm is raging and the winds of a bad report are causing you to feel unstable, speak the name of Jesus over your situation. Simply call upon the "Prince of Peace". He is already at rest concerning this storm (Matthew 8:24).

He reminds you, "Enter My rest. Enter the strong tower which is My Name. You are safe."
Thank you, Jesus.

<u>Prayer</u>

"Lord, I receive Your peace. It is a gift from You that I will not give away. No matter what I see or hear, I let Your peace guard my mind and heart. I am confident in <u>Your</u> ability."

<u>Jesus' Words that Point to this Commandment</u>

Luke 24:36-39, John 14:27, John 16:33, John 20:19,21,26

> *Jesus said, "I am leaving you with a gift—peace of mind and heart! And the peace I give isn't fragile like the peace the world gives. So, don't be troubled or afraid."*
> *John 14:27 TLB*

How can I apply this to my life?

____

____

____

____

____

____

"Everything I have taught you is so that the peace which is in Me will be in you and will give you great confidence as you rest in Me. For in this unbelieving world you will experience trouble and sorrows, but you must be courageous, for I have overcome the world."-Jesus

John 16:33 TPT

Don't Require Any Payment in God's House. I Paid the Only Price for Righteousness.

Red Letters

Jesus put together a whip out of strips of leather and chased them (the fraudulent merchants) out of the Temple, stampeding the sheep and cattle, upending the tables of the loan sharks, spilling coins left and right. He told the dove merchants, "Get your things out of here! Stop turning my Father's house into a shopping mall!" That's when his disciples remembered the Scripture, "Zeal for your house consumes me."
John 2:16-17 MSG

The merchants outside the temple were selling things that the temple leaders said were required by the people for sacrifice. The only place the people could buy these things was at the temple, so the merchants marked their prices as high as they wanted.

The moneychangers were also cheating the people when they came to the great temple from far-away places and had to change their currency. Those that wanted to worship were being gouged by the temple.

This fueled God's anger - the place where God wanted to bring wholeness to His people was stripping and misusing them. Jesus said, "No!"

You do not need to be perfect to go to church. You do not need to wear special clothing or pay special fees. Jesus paid it all for you to stand before the Lord as the righteousness of God (2 Corinthians 5:21).

Come as you are, ask forgiveness, and enter His Holy place. He wants to make you whole.

Offer your sacrifice of praise and be ready to receive every good and perfect gift from Him!

Prayer

"Lord, I forgive those who have hurt me at church. I will come into your house of worship and receive every good and perfect gift You have for me. Help me to welcome all who feel used by religion and show them the Love of God."

Jesus' Words that Point to this Commandment

Matthew 21:12-16, Mark 11:15-17, John 2:16-17

Jesus told them, "It is written in the Scriptures, 'My Temple is to be a place of prayer for all nations,' but you have turned it into a den of robbers." Mark 11:17

How can I apply this to my life?

____

____

____

____

____

____

You shall walk after the Lord your God and you shall fear [and worship] Him [with awe-filled reverence and profound respect], and you shall keep His commandments and you shall listen to His voice, and you shall serve Him, and cling to Him.

Deuteronomy 13:4 AMP

Be Kind.

Red Letters

Jesus said, "Love your enemies and do good and lend, hoping for nothing again: and your reward shall be great, and ye shall be the children of the highest: for He is kind unto the thankful and the unthankful and to the evil." Luke 6:35 KJV

Be kind and you will be known as a child of God.

God, your Father, sends life-giving rain on the bad and the good.
He sent His son to die for all men. Be generous like He is generous.

His great kindness showered you with mercy. When you became His, He crowned you with loving-kindness. Your ability to be kind to others comes from spending time in His Presence, being filled with His love for you. Let His mercy flow freely from you.

This goes contrary to earthly wisdom which says you should do good to those who are good to you. Make sure you are following God's wisdom and not the world's.

Proverbs (the book of wisdom) says, "Do not let kindness and truth leave you; bind them around your neck, write them on the tablet of your heart. You will find favor in the sight of God and man" (Proverbs 3:3-4).

Jesus commands you to bless your enemies and do good to those who have done you evil. If this seems hard to do, remember when you honor God with this commandment His blessings, according to Deuteronomy 28:2, "will overtake you."

That person, whom you consider an enemy, will be forced to pause and wonder from where you draw your great strength, and God will be glorified.

Prayer

"Lord, give me wisdom to plan my day. Help me not be so rushed I forget to be kind. You have been so kind and patient with me. I follow You in this. I will be kind to the sick, the sinners, the forgotten ones, and even those who do not deserve my kindness."

Jesus' Words that Point to this Commandment

Matthew 5:43-48, Matthew 25:35-36, Luke 6:31-36,43-45, Luke 10:30-37, John 13:34-35, John 17:20-23

> *Jesus said, "You're familiar with the old written law, 'Love your friend,' and its unwritten companion, 'Hate your enemy.' I'm challenging that. I'm telling you to love your enemies. Let them bring out the best in you, not the worst. When someone gives you a hard time, respond with the energies of prayer, for then you are working out of your true selves, your God-created selves. This is what God does. He gives his best—the sun to warm and the rain to nourish—to everyone, regardless: the good and bad, the nice and nasty. If all you do is love the lovable, do you expect a bonus? Anybody can do that. If you simply say hello to those who greet you, do you expect a medal? Any run-of-the-mill sinner does that. In a word, what I'm saying is, Grow up. You're kingdom subjects. Now live like it. Live out your God-created identity. Live generously and graciously toward others, the way God lives toward you."*
>
> *Matthew 5:43-50 MSG*

How can I apply this to my life?

____

____

____

Daily, Look to the Cross. You Will Live.

Red Letters

Jesus said unto her, "I am the resurrection, and the life: he that believeth in me, though he were dead, yet shall he live."
John 11:25 KJV

In the days of Moses, the snakes of the desert were killing the Israelites, so Moses, led by God, put a fiery bronze serpent on a stick and raised it up. When anyone was bitten by a snake, they would look to the bronze serpent on the stick and live.

This was a foreshadowing of Jesus on the cross.
He became a curse in place of the curses meant for us.

Christ redeemed us from sin, sickness and a self-defeating, cursed life by absorbing it completely into himself. There is an Old Testament scripture that says, "Cursed is everyone who hangs on a tree." That is what happened when Jesus was nailed to the cross: He became a curse, and at the same time dissolved the curse. And now, because of that, the air is cleared, and we can see that Abraham's blessing (success in every area of life) is present and available for all. We are able to receive God's life, his Spirit, in and with us by believing (Galatians 3:13 MSG).

When you are sick, look to the cross. When you are in torment, look to the cross. When you have a need, look to the cross. When you are in the valley of death, set your eyes on the cross.
When you do, believe, and you will live.

The cross is the "door" to life. When you enter that door by believing, the enemy will not be able to destroy you.

Prayer

"Lord, I look to the cross, today, for healing in my body, peace in my soul, and forgiveness for all my sin. I stand in the shadow of the cross, the shadow of the Almighty, who's power no enemy can withstand. When I do, Your salvation washes over me."

Jesus' Words that Point to this Commandment

John 3:14-18, John 11:25-26, John 12:31-33

Jesus said, "Just as Moses lifted up the snake in the wilderness, so the Son of Man must be lifted up, that everyone who believes may have eternal life in him." John 3:14-15 NIV

How can I apply this to my life?

____

____

____

____

____

Jesus said, "These words I speak to you are not incidental additions to your life, homeowner improvements to your standard of living... They are foundational words, words to build a life on. If you work these words into your life, you are like a smart carpenter who built his house on solid rock. Rain poured down, the river flooded, a tornado hit–but nothing moved that house. It was fixed to the rock."

Matthew 7:24 MSG

Die to Self.

Red Letters

Then Jesus said to all, "Anyone who wants to follow me must put aside his own desires and conveniences and carry his cross with him every day and keep close to me!"
Luke 9:23 TLB

This sounds harsh, but it is an important part of being a follower of Jesus. You must carry your own cross in life which means to deny your self-centered needs and put to death your fleshly desires.
They block the gentle voice of your Shepherd.

To be clear, we care for our bodies, but we are not moved by the impulses of our body. Our emotions can inform us, but we are not moved by our emotions. Your spirit, led by the Holy Spirit, must be the "decider" in your life.

See this "dying to yourself" as planting a seed. When a fruit dies and falls to the earth, it begins to rot below the tree. When it dissolves into the soil, seeds are released. Without the fruit decomposing, the seeds would not germinate and create more life.
Like the fruit, when you release your fleshly needs and desires, your life can produce seed that gives way to others coming to eternal life through Jesus.

When we are walking in the peace of God, we are in alignment. Our spirit is being led by the Holy Spirit and our body and soul (emotions, reasoning, and will) are listening to our spirit.
"The mature believer is led by the impulses of the Holy Spirit" Romans 8:14 TPT.

Make it a habit to ask daily, "Lord, what are YOUR purposes and plans for my day?"

Prayer

"Lord, forgive me for putting myself first. I give you my life. Your understanding is so much higher than mine. You know what I need. I take pleasure in my relationship with You and because of this, You will bring my heart's desires to pass."

Jesus' Words that Point to this Commandment

John 12:24-28, Luke 9:23, Matthew 10:38, Mark 8:34, Matthew 16:24

> *Jesus said, "Very truly I tell you, unless a kernel of wheat falls to the ground and dies, it remains only a single seed. But if it dies, it produces many seeds. Anyone who loves their life will lose it, while anyone who hates their life in this world will keep it for eternal life. Whoever serves me must follow me; and where I am, my servant also will be. My Father will honor the one who serves me."*
>
> *John 12:24-26 NIV*

How can I apply this to my life?

____

____

____

____

____

____

____

____

Know God's Will. Discern Your Situation.

Red Letters

Follow Me in this:

Jesus said, *"Now is my soul troubled; and what shall I say? 'Father, save me from this hour': but for this cause came I unto this hour."*

John 12:27 KJV

When you are faced with trouble, don't be quick to decide the best outcome for that situation. Stop and pray. Take a moment to seek the Father's will and ask, "How should I pray, Lord?"

When you are directed by the Holy Spirit on how to pray, it will fill you with faith. Your prayer will be in-agreement with God's perfect plan which will make it highly effective.

"If any of you lacks wisdom, let him ask God, who gives generously to all without reproach, and it will be given him" (James 1:5 ESV).

When faced with His crucifixion, our Savior had the power to change His situation instantly, but He knew God's will. He needed to give His life for the sins of all mankind.

Follow Jesus, seek God's will, and be prepared to surrender to it. Desire to have your life align with God's will.

If you are unable to hear His voice clearly in the moment, remember, His Word is always His will. Go to His Word for direction and pray the promises of God.

Our prayers are not answered only to meet our needs, but to glorify God.

Prayer

"Lord, let Your will be done in my life. I surrender my will to You. Any burning desire I have that is not from You, let it burn out. Kindle the fire of the Holy Spirit in me."

Jesus' Words that Point to this Commandment

Matthew 7:21-23, Matthew 26:53-54, John 4:34, John 6:38, John 7:17, John 12:27-28

> *"My food," said Jesus, "is to do the will of him who sent me and to finish his work." John 4:34*

How can I apply this to my life?

____

____

____

____

____

____

Give me an understanding heart so that I can passionately know and obey Your truth. Guide me into the paths that please You, for I take delight in all that You say. Cause my heart to bow before Your words of wisdom and not to the wealth of this world...
Drench my soul with life as I walk in Your path.

Psalm 119:35-37

Speak God's Victorious Word Over Every Area of Your Life.

Red Letters

Follow Me in this:

Jesus said, "The voice didn't come for me but for you. At this moment the world is in crisis. Now Satan, the ruler of this world, will be thrown out. And I, as I am lifted up from the earth, will attract everyone to me and gather them around me." He put it this way to show how he was going to be put to death. John 12:31-33 MSG

Jesus' eyes were on His victory. He spoke the Word of God with authority. When Jesus rose from the dead, every word He spoke rose with Him.

When you speak the Word of God, His authority comes on the scene. The Word rises above every circumstance. His Word is filled with victorious promises for every area of your life. Seek them out. Write them down. Make it a daily habit to speak God's promises over your life.

The Word of God spoken by a believer is sharper than a double-edged sword. One of those sword edges cuts the power of evil to harm you, the other edge cuts the sin out of your life that weakens you. The Word is a powerful weapon.

Your life is steered by your words (James 3:3-5). If you keep speaking words of defeat and lack over your life, your life will very soon reflect those words (Proverbs 18:21). If you speak the Living Word over your life, you will begin to walk toward all the good promises God has for you here on earth.

Sometimes changes come slowly, but your eye is now on the prize. You begin to act victorious because you are looking into God's eyes, and the small annoyances stop ruling over you.

Jesus was walking into the darkest moment of His life, but His eye was on the end result: His victory.

Don't let life roll over you, overcome like He did with the victorious Word of God.

Prayer

"Lord, I choose to speak Your words of life over everything that concerns me. According to Proverbs 18:21, the power of life and death is on my tongue.Let it be recorded that today, I choose life."

Jesus' Words that Point to this Commandment

Matthew 12:34-37, Mark 11:23, Luke 6:45, John 1:1-3, John 12:31

Jesus said, "Truly I tell you, if anyone says to this mountain, 'Go, throw yourself into the sea,' and does not doubt in their heart but believes that what they say will happen, it will be done for them." Mark 11:23 NIV

How can I apply this to my life?

____

____

____

____

____

____

Heaven and earth will pass away but My words will not pass away.

Mark 13:31

Don't Return to Dark Habits.

Red Letters

Jesus said, "I have come as a Light to shine in this dark world, so that all who put their trust in me will no longer wander in the darkness."
John 12:46 TLB

Where Jesus is, there is life-giving Light.
If your life has taken a turn and darkness surrounds you, return to the Light.

When a believer chooses to enter darkness after being in the Light, they will want to hide with their sin. It isn't the condemnation of the Lord that keeps them away from Him, it is their own self-condemnation.

Conviction is a wonderful gift of the Holy Spirit. But condemnation is a work of the darkness. Conviction says, "You are going in the wrong direction. Turn back and get back on the right path." Condemnation says, "You messed up. You always mess up. Walking on the right path is impossible for you."

Jesus says, "I am the Light. Turn your heart toward Me. Let my Light cover you and guide you away from the darkness. Let's start again."

Repent, receive God's grace (undeserved blessing), come into the Light and you will start doing God inspired things.

These things will bring a harvest of blessing on your life.
And this change of atmosphere is one prayer away.

Where there is light, darkness cannot exist.

Prayer

"Lord, thank you for Your grace. Your strength is made perfect in my weakness. You forgive all of my sins and heal me of all my diseases. I enter into Your glorious light!"

Jesus' Words that Point to this Commandment

John 3:17-21, John 8:12, John 9:5, John 11:9-10, John 12:35-36, John 12:46

> *Jesus said, "This is the crisis we're in: God-light streamed into the world, but men and women everywhere ran for the darkness. They went for the darkness because they were not really interested in pleasing God. Everyone who makes a practice of doing evil, addicted to denial and illusion, hates God-light and won't come near it, fearing a painful exposure. But anyone working and living in truth and reality welcomes God-light so the work can be seen for the God-work it is." John 3:19-21 MSG*

How can I apply this to my life?

Don't Judge Others. It's Not Your Job.

Red Letters

Follow Me in this:

Soon a Samaritan woman came to draw water, and Jesus asked her for a drink. He was alone at the time as his disciples had gone into the village to buy some food. The woman was surprised that a Jew would ask a "despised Samaritan" for anything—usually they wouldn't even speak to them! And she remarked about this to Jesus. He replied, "If you only knew what a wonderful gift God has for you, and who I am, you would ask me for some living water!"

John 4:7-10 TLB

When you come upon a situation where there are people you do not know, what do you do?

Most people assess or judge quickly. Through association we place people in social circles and through initial impressions, we judge who they were, who they are, and who they will be.

Your Savior wants you to give up the habit of "criticizing and judging others", and then He says, "you will not be criticized and judged in return" (Luke 6:37). He also says, "Stop judging based on the superficial. First you must embrace the standards of mercy and truth" (John 7:24 TPT).

Follow Jesus and love people first. You don't want to be put in a labeled box, neither do they. And don't be in a hurry. Listen to their story.
Be like Jesus and tell them about God's gift.

Never get caught up in pride and see others lower than you. Jesus was the only one who COULD sit in the seat of judgement and He chose to focus, instead, on making sure all men would come to God through His gift. Make that your focus too.

Prayer

"Jesus, help me to be more like You. I lay criticism at your throne. I let go of the need to judge others. Give me Your eyes for those who are in need. Help me see everyone through the lens of Your mercy and truth."

Jesus' Words that Point to this Commandment

Matthew 7:1-5, Matthew 7:12, Luke 6:31-42, Luke 10:30-37, Luke 19:1-10, John 3:17, John 4:7-30, John 7:24, John 8:1-8, John 12:47-48, John 13:34-35

Jesus said, "If anyone hears me and doesn't obey me, I am not his judge—for I have come to save the world and not to judge it."
John 12:47 TLB

How can I apply this to my life?

____

____

____

____

____

My child, pay attention to what I say. Listen carefully to my words. Don't lose sight of them. Let them penetrate deep into your heart, for they bring life to those who find them, and healing to their whole body.

Proverbs 4:20-22 NLT

Let Me Satisfy Your Spiritual Thirst.

Red Letters

Jesus said, "All you thirsty ones, come to Me! Come to Me and drink! Believe in Me so that rivers of living water will burst out from within you, flowing from your innermost being, just like the scripture says!"
John 7:37-38 TPT

From birth, your soul is thirsty.
Remember, your needs are not just physical. Your spirit-man needs spiritual "water". Jesus says He is the source of that "Living Water".

All of the world's attempts to satisfy this thirst will fail.
His Water satisfies your spirit and soul, eternally. It will satisfy you forever.

Hopelessness is a symptom of spiritual thirst. Jesus came to quench that thirst. *"Christ (is) in you, the hope of glory"* (Colossians 1:27).

We see a foreshadowing of this water when the Israelites were thirsty during their Exodus from Egypt. They were in the middle of the desert and desperately needed water to drink. Led by the Lord, Moses hit the rock and cool water burst forth.

Jesus is our Rock (Acts 4:11). He satisfies our desperate thirst and we are saved.

If you find yourself spiritually dry, go to the Word. Jesus IS the Word (John 1:14). The living water of the Word will wash you and refresh you.

The truth discovered in the scriptures will satisfy the weakest, most thirsty soul, transforming him into a river that pours out living water to everyone he meets.

Prayer

"Lord, wash me with Your Word. Fill me with Your Living Water so that out of my spirit will flow a river of revelation and life.
Everyone I meet will know I have Your life-giving water."

Jesus' Words that Point to this Commandment

Matthew 5:6, John 4:13-14, John 6:35,53-58,63, John 7:37-39

> *Jesus replied, "I am the Bread of Life. No one coming to me will ever be hungry again. Those believing in me will never thirst."*
> *John 6:35 TLB*

How can I apply this to my life?

____

____

____

____

____

____

____

____

____

He sends His word and melts them: He stirs up His breezes, and the waters flow. Psalm 147:18 NIV

Let Your Good Works Define You.

Red Letters

Jesus said, "Let your light so shine before men, that they may see your good works, and glorify your Father which is in Heaven."
Matthew 5:16 KJV

Picture a dark stadium filled with thousands of people staring into the darkness. Suddenly one person lights a candle.

Every eye in that stadium would instantly be drawn to that light. It would illuminate the person holding it and those around him or her. People would not be able to look away. They would study the person with the light and every detail around them.

Hold the light of Jesus Christ up in every area of your life.
All of creation yearns for the light of Christ in you to shine. Be different. They will know you are a Christian because of your love for Christ, your love for His words, and your love for others.

Love will always be the source of this supernatural light.

Stand up for Christ even when darkness is all around.
Don't fade into the darkness. Your good works will bring light.

Eyes will be on you even when you are unaware.

And we never shine to be seen. We shine because we reflect the love of Jesus. In the end, God will be glorified through your life.

Prayer

"Lord, help me shine Your light without fear. Help me to burn bright with Your love. My ears are open today to hear Your voice, leading me to good works."

Jesus' Words that Point to this Commandment

Matthew 4:23-25, Matthew 5:14-16, Matthew 6:3-4, Matthew 19:1-2, Luke 8:16-18, Luke 11:33-36, Luke 12:2-3, John 3:19-21, John 5:35-36, John 8:12, John 9:5, John 11:9-10, John 12:36, John 12:45-46

> *Jesus said, "For a brief time still, the light is among you. Walk by the light you have so darkness doesn't destroy you. If you walk in darkness, you don't know where you're going. As you have the light, believe in the light. Then the light will be within you and shining through your lives. You'll be children of light."*
>
> *John 12:36 MSG*

How can I apply this to my life?

____

____

____

____

____

Write these commandments that I've given you today on your hearts. Get them inside of you and then get them inside your children. Talk about them wherever you are, sitting at home or walking in the street; talk about them from the time you get up in the morning to when you fall into bed at night. Deuteronomy 6:6-7 MSG

Feed Your Faith with God's Word.

Red Letters

Jesus answered by quoting Deuteronomy: "It takes more than bread to stay alive. It takes a steady stream of words from God's mouth."
Matthew 4:4 MSG

"In the beginning was the Word, and the Word was with God, and the Word was God" (John 1:1).

Have you ever wanted to sit face to face with your Creator and hear His wisdom concerning life? His wisdom is in His Word and it is available to you every day. Search it, meditate on it, receive it as you would a meal. Let it enter you and bring strength to your faith.

His Word *IS* His Presence. In Hebrews 9:2 it states that the holy chamber inside the tabernacle (the sacred dwelling place of God) held the "lampstand (light) and the bread of His Presence on the fellowship table". The bread of His Presence is His Word and it is the holiest element we can eat.

The bread of His Word brings revelation. We taste the revelation of the goodness of God. The more we understand who God is and who we are, our faith is strengthened.

If you skipped eating food for days, your body would weaken. Likewise, going without reading scripture will weaken your spirit-man.

This weakness will carry over to your mind, your will and your emotions. Addictions will strengthen, weariness will tempt you to give up, and faith will walk out as fatigue walks in.

God's Word will strengthen you. It will remind you of who you are in Christ and this knowledge will make you a champion.

Prayer

"Lord, I am hungry for Your promises. I am hungry to know Your ways and Your solutions. I want to eat the Bread of Your Presence found in Your Word. Thank you for the strength that comes when I read Your Word and enjoy the Bread of Life."

Jesus' Words that Point to this Commandment

Matthew 4:4, Matthew 7:7-11, Matthew 22:1-14, Matthew 26:26-28, Mark 14:22-25, Luke 4:4,8,12, John 1:1-14, John 6:27-35, 47-58, John 21:15-17

And Jesus answered him, saying, "It is written, that man shall not live by bread alone, but by every word of God."
Luke 4:4 KJV

How can I apply this to my life?

____

____

____

____

____

____

When I discovered Your words, I devoured them.
They are my joy and my heart's delight,
for I bear Your Name, O Lord God of Heaven's armies.
Jeremiah 15:16 NLT

Do Not Give Your Body to Anyone but the Person You Married.

Red Letters

Jesus said, "*You know the next commandment pretty well, too: 'Don't go to bed with another's spouse.' But don't think you've preserved your virtue simply by staying out of bed. Your heart can be corrupted by lust even quicker than your body. Those leering looks you think nobody notices—they also corrupt.*"

Matthew 5:28 MSG

Faithfulness toward your husband or wife begins in your thoughts. Do not let your mind imagine being with someone other than your spouse. This opens the door to sin and its destruction.

The seed of all sin begins in the thought life. Develop self-discipline in your thought life by replacing dark imaginings with God's Word.

If you are not married, God has your desires on His heart. Keep pure and practice faithfulness now. Trust Him to lead you to your blessing.

And remember, His love and forgiveness are always available, and he wants to heal your heart. He wants to crown you with loving-kindness and tender mercies.

You do not go this alone. You have a friend and Savior in Jesus who will never leave you. When lust sends a bolt through your heart, begin to praise God. Your praise will change the atmosphere. It will grab hold of the reins on your heart. The Helper will enter and give you wisdom and direction. He will remind you that God will meet all of your needs through His heavenly riches and His powerful glory.

Today, make the choice to think righteously and your life will be blessed.

Prayer

"Father, forgive me for giving away what You have called precious. I receive Your forgiveness. I surrender every lie I have believed that is fueled by lust. I am more than my body. You are the Lord of my life. I lay this at your throne. I take every thought captive. Thank you for giving me what is perfect. I will not settle for anything less."

Jesus' Words that Point to this Commandment

Matthew 5:8, Matthew 5:27-28,29-30, Mark 7:20-23, John 8:34

> *And then Jesus added, "It is the thought-life that pollutes. For from within, out of men's hearts, come evil thoughts of lust, theft, murder, adultery, wanting what belongs to others, wickedness, deceit, lewdness, envy, slander, pride, and all other folly. All these vile things come from within; they are what pollute you and make you unfit for God."*
>
> *Mark 7:20-23 TLB*

How can I apply this to my life?

Do not Steal.

Red Letters

Jesus said,

"Thou shalt not steal." Matthew 19:18 KJV

Remember, God can and will provide your every need.
Stealing is a lack of faith that God will take care of you.

"They'll never know. They have so much. They can spare it."
These might sound reasonable in the moment, but they are part of a trap. Stealing something will always open the door to something being stolen from you.

The enemy of your soul is waiting for your choice. When you steal, you open the door for him to steal, kill, and destroy anything that concerns you (John 10:10).
This is a serious matter.

Your obedience will allow Jesus to usher in abundant life. He wants you to prosper and succeed. The Holy Spirit said it this way in the book of Ephesians: "If any one of you has stolen from someone else, never do it again. Instead, be industrious, earning an honest living and then you'll have enough to bless those in need" (Ephesians4:28 TPT).
Stealing always leaves you empty and keeps you locked in a place of lack.

Which is right where the enemy wants you.

Close the door to the thief.

Prayer

"Lord, I trust you will meet all of my needs. I receive Your freedom from the love of money. Help me to look for opportunities to give and not take. I receive your abundant life. I receive a peaceful life and the ability to live in confident rest."

Jesus' Words that Point to this Commandment

Matthew 7:7, Matthew 19:18-19, Mark 10:19, Luke 12:33-34, Luke 18:19-20, John 10:1-5,7-11

> *Jesus said, "The thief cometh not, but for to steal, and to kill, and to destroy: I am come that they might have life, and that they might have it more abundantly."*
> *John 10:10 KJV*

How can I apply this to my life?

____

____

____

____

____

____

____

____

Oh, how kind our Lord was, for he showed me how to trust him and become full of the love of Christ Jesus. 1 Timothy 1:14 TLB

Beware of Envy: Do Not Let the Desire for What Belongs to Someone Else Enter Your Heart.

Red Letters

Jesus said, "Take care! Protect yourself against the least bit of greed. Life is not defined by what you have, even when you have a lot."
Luke 12:15 MSG

Don't let envy into your heart. When jealousy and envy enter in, they bring disorder to your mind. This allows depression to settle on your thoughts.

Always remember, a man or woman's life is not defined by the abundance of things they possess.
Your joy will never be completed by possessions.

The spirit of envy will try to deceive you into thinking if you possess that object, it will bring satisfaction, peace, joy, comfort, power, or honor. Don't be deceived, these are NEVER the result of possession.

Instead, go to your Heavenly Father in prayer.
Just one moment in His Presence will bring rest to your soul.
His Fatherly love is there to bless you with your desires and to show you the way to your blessing.

Meditate on this truth: You have Jesus.
He has promised, "I will never leave you or forsake you."
He is the King of all kings. He is the Lord of all lords. His personal Presence over you brings the blessing of wealth.

In His blessing there is nothing missing. According to the book of Wisdom, "The blessing of the Lord makes rich, and He adds no sorrow with it" (Proverbs 10:22) Thank you, Jesus.

Prayer

"Lord, You are my provider. My job is to seek You today and all these things will be added to my life. As my soul prospers, so will everything that concerns me. You have made me a giver and I will always have more than enough. Thank you in advance for all you are doing in my life."

Jesus' Words that Point to this Commandment

Mark 7:21-23, Luke 12:15-21, John 14:1, John 16:13-15

Jesus said,
"Let not your heart be troubled: ye believe in God, believe also in me." John 14:1 KJV

How can I apply this to my life?

____

____

____

____

____

____

____

My people shall sit in the beauty of peace, and in the tabernacles of confidence, and in wealthy rest. Isaiah 32:18 (Douay-Rheims)

Do Not Put Your Trust in Anything or Anyone Other Than Almighty God.

Red Letters

Jesus' refusal was curt: "Beat it, Satan!" He backed his rebuke with a third quotation from Deuteronomy: "Worship the Lord your God, and only him. Serve him with absolute single-heartedness."

Matthew 4:10 MSG

In the above scripture the enemy was telling Jesus,
"I will give you all these things if you will worship me."
Stop right here and ask yourself this question: "Who is my source?"

Who do you look to for your needs? Who has the power to give you a place of honor? Is it your job, the government, an association, your parents, your spouse, a friend, your children, your pastor...?

The only One who is reliable and able is Almighty God. He is your truth, ability, and strength.

The breath in your lungs is a gift from Him. The sun that rose this morning was His choice. The gravity that holds your feet on earth was spoken into existence by Him and not only that, He placed the earth itself in the vast darkness of space and it hasn't moved.

Everything that has life pulsating through it originated in His imagination.
It is amazing He even needs to ask us to put our trust in Him.

Beware of placing power into anyone's hands other than Almighty God to meet your needs.

God is your source and He is well able. He never changes. Make a firm decision to trust Him.

Today is the day for you to "trust in the Lord with all of your heart and not to lean on your own understanding. In all of your ways acknowledge Him and He will direct your paths" (Proverbs 3:5).

Prayer

"Father, you are my source. My help comes from the Creator of all things. You are able! Bless you, Almighty God! You hold the universe in Your hand, and You love me. Bless me! Your plans for me and my household are good."

Jesus' Words that Point to this Commandment

Matthew *4:1-11, Mark 9:23-24, Mark 11:22-24, Luke 10:27, Luke 12:22-32, John 16:23-24*

> *Jesus said, "Until now you've not been bold enough to ask the Father for a single thing in My name, but now you can ask, and keep on asking Him! And you can be sure that you'll receive what you ask for, and your joy will have no limits!"*
>
> *John 16:23-24 TPT*

How can I apply this to my life?

____

____

____

____

____

____

Love God's Name
And Use It ONLY for Addressing Him and His Power.

Red Letters
Jesus said, "Pray along these lines: *Our Father in Heaven,* *we honor your Holy Name."* *Matthew 6:9 TLB*

When you call upon God in prayer, He will hear you. Never use His name flippantly and certainly not as a curse. You must have honor for His name for your own sake.

Our own hearts must know He hears us when we call.

There is great power in the name of God. The Jewish people have such honor for His name they do not spell it out. It is not out of fear, but reverence.

In the book of Proverbs, His name is revealed as a place of perfect refuge (Proverbs 18:10). But we must have knowledge of the power and the authority of His name.

Study the names of God (several are listed on Page 314). Allow the revelation of the Names of the Almighty to take hold of your heart. When you address Him in prayer by these names, your faith will strengthen and your intimacy with Him will become richer.

We serve a personal God who wants to show you the heart of a loving Father, but we also serve the One whose name is above every name ever named (Philippians 2:9), in Whom every family in heaven and earth is named (Ephesians 3:15).

Prayer

"Jesus, Your name means the One who saves. Save me. It means the One who heals. Heal me. Your name is holy to me and I will honor it. Your name is above all names in Heaven, on the earth, and under the earth. I call Your name and You answer me. Thank you for your faithfulness. Bless Your Holy name!"

Jesus' Words that Point to this Commandment

Matthew 6:9, Luke 11:2, John 17:6

No using the name of God, your God, in curses or silly banter; God won't put up with the irreverent use of his name.
Exodus 20:7 MSG

How can I apply this to my life?

____

____

____

____

____

____

____

____

"I've loved you the way my Father has loved Me.
Make yourselves at home in My love. If you keep My commands,
you'll remain intimately at home in My love. That's what I've done–
kept My Father's commands and made Myself at home in His love"
-Jesus. John 15:9 MSG

Love God with All of Your Strength.

> *Red Letters*
>
> *Jesus said,*
> *"You are to love the Lord Yahweh, your God, with every passion of your heart, with all the energy of your being, with every thought that is within you, and with all your strength.*
> *This is the great and supreme commandment."*
> *Mark 12:30 TPT*

Loving God begins with knowing His voice. His voice is in the scriptures.

God revealed Himself most clearly in Jesus, who is the Word of God made flesh. When you meditate on His Word, you begin to understand the heart of God. You become intimately acquainted with His ways.

His Word fills your thought life so that your reactions begin to be filtered through God's Word. More and more you make decisions to be obedient to His Word in difficult circumstances.
You are loving God through your obedience.

What are those things that you are exceptional at doing? Love God with them.
What are you passionate about? Love God with all your passions.

Develop a prayer life that is a continuous conversation with God throughout the day. Practice being aware of His Presence in every moment.

Love Him with your self-control.
Love Him with your finances by supporting the causes He loves.

Love God in the morning when you are filled with strength.
Love God with your time.
Love God when it is not popular. Love God when you are feeling weak.

You are called to love Him with everything that you call your own, nothing reserved. As a result, everything that concerns your life will be wrapped in God. Perfection will be released into every part of your being until there is nothing missing and nothing lacking: Shalom.

__Prayer__

"I love you, Lord! Let every breath I breathe be for Your glory. You have turned my mourning into joy, my ashes into a thing of beauty and You have covered me with a robe of righteousness that makes me a child of the Most High. Let everything that is in me bless You Lord!"

__Jesus' Words that Point to this Commandment__

Matthew 6:24, Matthew 22:37, Mark 12:30, Luke 10:27

> *Jesus said,*
> *"Those who truly love Me are those who obey my commands. Whoever passionately loves Me will be passionately loved by My Father. And I will passionately love you in return and will manifest My life within you."*
> *John 14:21 MSG*

How can I apply this to my life?

____

____

____

____

____

Don't Sin.

Red Letters

Jesus said,

"Go on your way. From now on, don't sin." John 8:11 MSG

Don't sin? Is it even possible?
When we look at the definition of sin, it does seem possible:
Sin is any willful disobedience that makes God grieve.

Its ancient definition is "the act or state of missing the mark."
Sin is a focus problem.

It often comes from a prideful place of knowing what is best for you.
Sin comes with the platitude, "I am doing what makes me happy."
But does it really?
In the end, sin draws you as far from happiness as you can be.

If a person or place keeps causing you to sin and fall away from God, cut it out of your life. Focus on Jesus.
When sin promises you something, Jesus has the real promise.
"Whoever trusts in his own mind is a fool, but he who walks in wisdom will be delivered" (Proverbs 28:26). Keep clean, my friend, for the Kingdom of God is available to you.

When you serve sin, you become its servant. It is a hellish master.

Prayer

"Father, I repent of missing the mark. I turn my eyes from my sin and turn to you. I look into Your loving eyes and allow You to search my heart. Forgive me. Thank You for forgiving me of my sin and healing

me of all my diseases. You crown me with loving-kindness and tender mercy."

<u>Jesus' Words that Point to this Commandment</u>

Matthew 4:17, Matthew 5:29-30, Mark 1:15, Mark 9:43-48, Luke 13:1-9, John 5:14-16, John 8:10-11, John 8:34-36

> *Jesus said,*
> *"If your right eye serves as a trap to ensnare you or is an occasion for you to stumble and sin, pluck it out and throw it away. It is better that you lose one of your members than that your whole body be cast into hell."*
> *Matthew 5:29 AMP*

How can I apply this to my life?

____

____

____

____

____

If you listen obediently to the Voice of God, your God,
and heartily obey all his commandments that I command you today,
God, your God, will place you on high above all the nations of the world.
All these blessings will come down on you and spread out beyond you
because you have responded to the Voice of God, your God:
God's blessing inside the city, God's blessing in the country;
God's blessing in your coming in, God's blessing in your going out.
Deuteronomy 28:1-6 MSG

Receive Your Freedom.

Red Letters

Jesus said,

"So, if the Son liberates you [makes you freemen], then you are really and unquestionably free." John 8:36 AMP

Why is it so hard for us to receive this as a commandment?

Somewhere in the history of the church, people got locked into the box of religion. Condemnation blinded leaders and so much of our identity was about the sin. But Jesus is saying, "I took your sin and grief and pain and death. This isn't who you are. You are free. If I have made you free, you are really free! Receive that freedom right now! Walk in the freedom I give you!"

What is holding you down right now? Jesus set you free from that pressure. Surrender it and receive your perfect freedom.

There are too many Christ-followers who are heavily burdened, and Jesus says they are free. Make a quality decision right now to accept His perfect freedom.

If you are walking a path of sin, get off of it. It leads to destruction. Make a choice to ask for forgiveness, turn around, and walk with Jesus in a wide-open space.

Your freedom will begin when you renew your mind to accepting this freedom. Your mind will continue to be renewed while meditating on God's promises.

It is not your circumstances that dictate your freedom. It is the Lord of your life that dictates whether you are free. He will guide you out of your circumstances.

Prayer

"Lord, I come to Your throne and ask You to take my chains. Take my burdens. Take the labels that have been put on me. Take the grief. Take the pain. Take the addictions. Take the self-condemnation. Take the unforgiveness. Take everything that has made me weary. I receive Your freedom. You have brought me to this wide-open place. Your freedom is mine."

Jesus' Words that Point to this Commandment

Luke 4:18, Luke 5:19-26, Luke 7:47-50, John 8: 31-36, John 8:51, John 10:9-11

> *Jesus said, "The Spirit of the Lord is upon me; he has appointed me to preach Good News to the poor; he has sent me to heal the brokenhearted and to announce that captives shall be released and the blind shall see, that the downtrodden shall be freed from their oppressors, and that God is ready to give blessings to all who come to him." He closed the book and handed it back to the attendant and sat down, while everyone in the synagogue gazed at him intently. Then he added, "These Scriptures came true today!"*
>
> *Luke 7:50 TLB*

How can I apply this to my life?

____

____

____

____

____

____

Be Good to Your Mom and Dad and Honor Them.

Red Letters

"But Jesus put it right back on them. "Why do you use your rules to play fast and loose with God's commands? God clearly says, 'Respect your father and mother,' and, 'Anyone denouncing father or mother should be killed.' But you weasel around that by saying, 'Whoever wants to, can say to father and mother, What I owed to you I've given to God.' That can hardly be called respecting a parent."

Matthew 15:3-4 MSG

This is the only commandment that comes with a specific promise: "It will be well with you and you will live long on the earth" (Deuteronomy 5:16). Now that is a wonderful promise!

God is a God of order. Parents come before children. Their lives gave entrance to your life. When children go before their parents, in any respect, there is chaos.

Your love and respect for your mother and father lay a foundation for the love and respect you have for your Heavenly Father.

For some this is an easy commandment. For others, it might be very difficult because of the nature of their parents. Don't be like the people Jesus referred to who manipulated this commandment.
Just do it. Even if your parents are not perfect, treat them respectfully.

Do it because Jesus commands you. You will experience a blessing over your soul. Isn't it wonderful that it is not your job to correct your parents, but rather to be a blessing to them. God will meet you there and will move on your behalf.

While suffering for the entire world and bearing the weight of all the sin of mankind on the cross, our Savior focused His attention for a moment to make sure His mother was taken care of (John 19:26).

Prayer

"Lord, thank you for my mother and father. Bless them today. Help me to treat them respectfully. I forgive them. Give me your wisdom so I can be a blessing to them."

Jesus' Words that Point to this Commandment

Matthew 15:1-8, Matthew 19:18-19, Mark 7:9-13, Mark 10:19, Luke 18:20, John 19:25-27

> *Now there stood by the cross of Jesus his mother...When Jesus therefore saw his mother, and the disciple standing by, whom he loved, he saith unto his mother, "Woman, behold thy son!" Then saith he to the disciple, "Behold thy mother!"*
> *And from that hour that disciple took her unto his own home.*
> *John 19:25-27 KJV*

How can I apply this to my life?

____

____

____

____

____

____

The precepts of the Lord are right, giving joy to the heart.
The commands of the Lord are radiant, giving light to the eyes.
Psalm 19:8 NIV

Be Prepared to Battle Against Darkness.

Red Letters

"Asleep!" Jesus said. "Get up! Pray God that you will not fall when you are tempted."
Luke 22:46 TLB

The enemy of God is your enemy and he is not asleep.
Do not be naive, the battle of good and evil surrounds you and you need to know how to defend yourself.

First of all, take up the armor of God (Read Ephesians 6:10-18). The very first weapon the enemy sends is doubt. Your battle will take place primarily in your mind. Take up the belt of Truth. It is your "core" support. Educate yourself in the Word. Know who God is, who your Savior is, and what you have been promised.

You placed the helmet of salvation on when you accepted Jesus as your Savior. It was a choice- never choose to take that helmet off. You do not need to work to keep that salvation on - it is your gift. Salvation encompasses protection for your spirit, soul, and body. The sharp accusations of the enemy will be repelled by the helmet of salvation.

If you have more faith in what you see than what the Word says, you will leave yourself exposed to the weapons of the enemy. Hold up your faith as a shield and walk by faith not by sight. Remind yourself of what Jesus taught you. Speak out loud what He promised you and Your shield will keep You protected.

In your mouth you hold a weapon of mass destruction. It is the spoken Word of God. The enemy has no defense against it. It destroys every plan, every lie, every stronghold he has set up. Speak God's promises over your situation and the enemy will retreat. Sometimes it takes a barrage of artillery, but it WILL take down all his defenses, if you do not quit. And remember, words that agree with the enemy's lies shatter YOUR defense.

After you have spoken God's word, speak your praises to Him. Spoken prayer, praying in your spiritual language, and words of praise confuse the enemy's plans (Read 2 Chronicles 20:20-22).

Lastly, stand. The moment you resist his temptations to sin, he runs in fear from you (James 4:7). Hold your ground.

Prayer

"Lord, reveal the strategies of the enemy in my life. I hear Your voice and follow You. I take authority over my enemy, in Jesus name. No weapon formed against me is allowed to prosper."

Jesus' Words that Point to this Commandment

Matthew 10:38, Matthew 16:18-19, Matthew 18:18-19, Matthew 26:41, Luke 10:18-19, Luke 11:20-23, Luke 22:31-32,40,46, John 10:10, John 16:31-33

> *Jesus said, "And I have given you authority over all the power of the Enemy, and to walk among serpents and scorpions and to crush them. Nothing shall injure you!"*
>
> *Luke 10:19 TLB*

How can I apply this to my life?

____

____

____

____

Make Going to Church Your Regular Habit.

Red Letters

Follow Me in this:

"And (Jesus) came to Nazareth, where he had been brought up: and, as his custom was, he went into the synagogue on the sabbath day, and stood up for to read."

Luke 4:16 KJV

If Jesus went to church regularly, you should too.
Fellowshipping with other believers is critical to being considered a follower of Jesus. You are called to share your spiritual gifts to strengthen others. Likewise, their gifts will strengthen you.

Your brothers and sisters in Christ will also keep you accountable so you do not justify sin.

Never believe that you will not be missed at your church no matter what size church you attend. You are there for a purpose and sometimes you do not know the lives you affect with one word or a smile. Even your presence could be the encouragement someone needs.

There is power when those who are filled with the Holy Spirit come together. Corporate worship is one the most important habits you can have. As a body, we are meant to be together because our strength is released in that atmosphere of agreement.

It is an environment where the love of God flows mightily. New revelations come forward that can change lives forever.

It has been recorded that when Christians gather as one body, they can change the spiritual climate of a city, and even a nation.

Prayer

"Lord, I love Your house of worship. I will take my place and do my part to make it strong. I will find goodness and mercy there and dwell in it all the days of my life."

Jesus' Words that Point to this Commandment

Matthew 4:10-11, Matthew 6:19-21,33, Matthew 16:18-19, Matthew 18:20, Matthew 26:26-30, Mark 1:21, Mark 3:1, Luke 4:16, Luke 6:6

As the believers met together that day, suddenly there was a sound like the roaring of a mighty windstorm in the skies above them and it filled the house where they were meeting.

Acts 2:1-2 TLB

How can I apply this to my life?

____

____

____

____

____

____

____

Do we love God? Do we keep his commands?

The proof that we love God comes when we keep his commandments and they are not at all troublesome.

1 John 5:3-4 MSG

Worship God with Your Whole Heart.

Red Letters

Jesus said, "God is Spirit, and those who worship Him must worship in spirit and truth."
John 4:24 NKJV

In the time when Jesus spoke these words, people would go through the motions of worship religiously. They would sway their robes a certain way and offer their words of praise, but their heart wasn't in it.

Jesus is teaching us that true worship is an act of the heart. It is not repeating what you see others do or saying holy phrases.

Study and know the God you worship. Know His authority, know His loving-kindness, and know His Fatherly guidance. Humble yourself and release all pride. Then allow your entire being to reflect your love for Him.

When you know His truth, you become a true worshipper.
The Father will seek those who are true worshippers.
When the Father seeks you out, life overflows with His goodness.

Jesus also knew that the key to living an overcoming life is in heartfelt worship. When you place God above your cares, above your circumstances, above your emotions, above your needs, above your hurts, and truly worship Him, He calls you to that high place in victory over the things of this world.

Prayer

"Lord, I worship You and honor You. I lift my hands to You and say,

You are the maker of Heaven and earth! You are the author and finisher of my faith. You reign forever and ever....and You love me!"

Jesus' Words that Point to this Commandment

Matthew 2:11, Matthew 6:5-13, Matthew 14:23, Matthew 15:8-9, Matthew 21:15-16, Matthew 18:3-4, Luke 4:8, Luke 10:19-20, Luke 18:10-14, John 4:21-24

> *Jesus said, "Therefore anyone who humbles himself as this little child is the greatest in the Kingdom of Heaven."*
> *Matthew 18:4 TLB*

How can I apply this to my life?

____

____

____

____

____

____

____

____

I long to drink of You, O God, drinking deeply from the streams of pleasure flowing from Your Presence. My longings overwhelm me for more of You! My soul thirsts, pants, and longs for the living God. I want to come and see the face of God.

Psalm 42:1-2 TPT

Don't Fear.

Red Letters

Jesus said, "But even the very hairs of your head are all numbered. Fear not, then; you are of more value than many sparrows."
Matthew 10:30-31 AMP

Jesus said over and over again during His earthly ministry, "Fear not... Don't be afraid... Just believe...Take courage, it is I... Don't be afraid." Remember, this is a commandment.

Your job is to resist fear. It is not an option. That spirit of fear is not from God. He has given you power in His name. He has given you perfect love to cast out fear. He has given you a sound mind to speak scripture over your situation.

In the world fear is accepted as a rational reaction. In the world people even seek fear for entertainment.
But Jesus knows fear will block the flow of God's anointing for healing, protection, and provision.

Don't ever be afraid, my friend. You are precious to God. He knows everything about you. Confidently know His love surrounds you.

Remember the words of Jesus, "Don't be afraid dearest friends! Your loving Father joyously gives you His kingdom realm with all its promises! (Luke 12:32 TPT)

Today you have a choice: Cling to what makes you anxious or cling to God.

Prayer

"Lord. I trust in You with all of my heart. I will not rely on my limited understanding concerning this situation. I choose to not yield to fear but instead I give all of my anxiety to You and receive Your perfect direction. Thank you for guiding me into Your answered prayer."

Jesus' Words that Point to this Commandment

Matthew 10:30-31, Mark 5:36, Mark 6:50, Luke 12:6-7, Luke 8:50, John 3:16, John 12:46, John 14:27

> *Jesus said, "Peace I leave with you; My [own] peace I now give and bequeath to you. Not as the world gives do I give to you. Do not let your hearts be troubled, neither let them be afraid. [Stop allowing yourselves to be agitated and disturbed; and do not permit yourselves to be fearful and intimidated and cowardly and unsettled.]"*
>
> *John 14:27 AMP*

How can I apply this to my life?

____

____

____

____

____

And a cloud threw a shadow upon them, and a voice came out of the cloud, saying, "This is My Son, the Beloved One. Be constantly listening to and obeying Him!"

Mark 9:7 AMP

Pray at All Times.

Red Letters

Follow Me in this:

"...With the crowd dispersed, he climbed the mountain, so he could be by himself and pray. He stayed there alone, late into the night."

Matthew 14:23 MSG

Your first act as a believer was to pray. So often, it happens, as we mature in our faith, our Christian works take precedence over prayer.
Make prayer a daily habit. Carve out a time where you will not be interrupted, distracted, or overheard. Don't play the part with empty repetitive prayers. Be real.

Prayer is not only about what you can receive from God, it is also a time to reveal yourself to your Heavenly Father. He will reveal Himself to you. Take the time to let His love and grace pour into you. Be silent, so you can listen. Then maintain a constant conversation with God throughout your day.

If your prayer life is not strong you will begin to lose heart and give up. Prayer is a lifeline to faith, and we know that with faith in God, all things are possible.

Pray at all times! Believe that God will justly defend and protect and avenge His people and He will do it quickly. The Holy Spirit instructs our hearts in 1 Thessalonians 5:16 (TPT) to, "Let joy be your continual feast. Make your life a prayer. And in the midst of everything be always giving thanks, for this is God's perfect plan for you in Christ Jesus." *This is God's perfect plan for you!*
The prayer of a righteous person is powerful and effective, and you are the righteousness of God in Christ Jesus (James 5:16). He hears you.

Prayer

"Father, I come to You. My heart is turned toward You. You call me friend. I repent, and You call me forgiven. I trust in you today and I will not trust in my own solutions. I pour every part of my heart out to you. I hear Your voice in my heart. I receive your wise counsel today."

Jesus' Words that Point to this Commandment

Matthew 5:44, Matthew 6:5-15, Matthew 9:38, Matthew 14:23, Matthew 21:21-22, Matthew 26:36-41, Matthew 26:53, Mark 1:35, Mark 6:46, Mark 9:29, Mark 11:24-26, Luke 5:16, Luke 18:1-8, Luke 18:35-43, John 17:9-19

> *One day Jesus told his disciples a story to illustrate their need for constant prayer and to show them that they must keep praying until the answer comes. "There was a city judge," he said, "a very godless man who had great contempt for everyone. A widow of that city came to him frequently to appeal for justice against a man who had harmed her. The judge ignored her for a while, but eventually she got on his nerves. "'I fear neither God nor man,' he said to himself, 'but this woman bothers me. I'm going to see that she gets justice, for she is wearing me out with her constant coming!'" Then the Lord said, "If even an evil judge can be worn down like that, don't you think that God will surely give justice to his people who plead with him day and night? Yes! He will answer them quickly! But the question is: When I, the Messiah, return, how many will I find who have faith and are praying?"*
>
> *Luke 18:1-8 TLB*

How can I apply this to my life?

____

____

____

____

Do Not Get Angry and Call People Names.

> *Red Letters*
>
> *Jesus said, "But I say to you that whoever is angry with his brother without a cause shall be in danger of the judgment. And whoever says to his brother, 'Raca!' (empty head) shall be in danger of the council. But whoever says, 'You fool!' shall be in danger of hell fire."*
>
> *Matthew 5:22 KJV*

Our culture sees nothing wrong with a harmless derogatory term for the guy who cuts you off on the highway. Jesus says it is not ok.

This is where you need to make the decision to follow Jesus or the world.

"Thou shalt not kill" can be an easy command to follow on a daily basis, but "Thou shalt not call someone an idiot," is not so easy! Jesus says it can put you in danger of Hell. Why? Because you are stepping out of the love of God and if you stay out there long enough you will sever your relationship with Him.

He is being very clear here. His commandments are for your well-being. Obey them and you will receive His peace and as a result, you will spread that peace wherever you go.

Your obedience will change the atmosphere like salt seasons food.

Prayer

"Lord, put a guard on my mouth. I will speak words that lift up and not put down. I will be diligent about what I chose to say. Help me be to be wise and keep my mouth shut."

Jesus' Words that Point to this Commandment

Matthew 5:22-26, Matthew 16:23-26, Mark 9:49-50, John 5:30, John 14:27

Jesus said, "Good salt is worthless if it loses its saltiness; it can't season anything. So, don't lose your flavor! Live in peace with each other." Mark 9:50 TLB

How can I apply this to my life?

____

____

____

____

____

____

____

____

____

Jesus replied,

"Loving Me empowers you to obey My word.

And My Father will love you so deeply that We will come to you and make you Our dwelling place.

But those who do not love Me will not obey My words. The Father did not send Me to speak my own revelation, but the words of My Father.

John 14:23 -24 TPT

Love Your Enemies and Bless Them That Curse You.

Red Letters

Jesus said, "Love your enemies, treat well (do good, act nobly toward) those who detest you and pursue you with hatred."

Luke 6:27 AMP

When your mind becomes set on retribution toward your enemy it consumes all of your thoughts.

Hatred replaces love. Frustration pushes away peace. The path of these thoughts leads to more pain and the original injury turns to anguish.

Jesus is commanding us to pray for our enemies and actually love them. What He is asking is, on a human level, impossible. This is where, in your walk to follow Jesus, you pick up your cross. The offences and hatred must be sacrificed. Inside of you, where your born-again spirit burns eternal, lives the victorious Spirit of the Living God. He is providing for you, right now, impossible love. Step aside and yield to His love: forgive them and pray for them.

Taking this action heals you, and it does more to frustrate your enemy than any retribution you could come up with. Your enemy might even change. The shame and anger that fuels them will be exposed.

There is something higher than human justice-it is God's justice.
Let go of this responsibility and let it be God's.

When we obey this commandment, Jesus says everyone will know we are our Father's child and as a bonus you will be overtaken with His blessing.

While they were nailing Jesus to the cross, He prayed over and over, 'Father forgive them, for they don't know what they are doing' (Luke 23:34 TPT).

Prayer

"Lord, I surrender my life to you. I surrender my enemies to you. You perfect everything that concerns me. You have promised me that you will defend my reputation. Jesus, I will follow you and say, 'Father, I forgive them'. I will not be governed by my anger, but I will be gentle because I honor You. I can do this because I am filled with Your love."

Jesus' Words that Point to this Commandment

Matthew 5:43-46, Mark 11:25-26, Luke 6:27-36

> *If thine enemy be hungry, give him bread to eat; and if he be thirsty, give him water to drink: For thou shalt heap coals of fire upon his head, and the Lord shall reward thee.*
>
> *Proverbs 25:21*

How can I apply this to my life?

___

___

___

___

My child, don't forget my law, but keep my commandments in your heart. They will give you a peaceful, long life. Keep them like a locket around your neck and engrave them in your heart. If you do this, you will have favor with God and with man...

Proverbs 3:1-4

Stay Married.

Red Letters

But Jesus said to them, "Because of your hardness of heart [your condition of insensibility to the call of God] he wrote you this precept in your Law (divorce). But from the beginning of creation God made them male and female. For this reason, a man shall leave [behind] his father and his mother and be joined to his wife and cleave closely to her permanently, and the two shall become one flesh, so that they are no longer two, but one flesh. What therefore God has united (joined together), let not man separate or divide." Mark 10:5-9

If you are married, divorce is not a solution for unhappiness. Marriage is a ministry where you are called to love, serve, and give to your spouse. When the focus reverses and your marriage is weighed on what you are receiving, the power of that union is weakened.

God designed marriage. The Creator made Adam and then Eve, and they were made to complement one another, physically and mentally. The differences they had individually equaled strength together. Their union created life and the Giver of Life took great pleasure in them.

The enemy of life took great disdain in them. Sometimes we need to look at what the enemy is violently against and determine that these are his greatest threats. He is against every aspect of marriage. The power of agreement between a man and a woman must be devastating to his plans.

Yield your marriage to the One who designed it. Don't get caught up in the world's idea of what marriage is and how to make it work.

You are not alone. Marriage was God's idea and He can help. But be ready to listen and obey His counsel.

Remember, God has blessed you in marriage as one flesh. How can you separate one flesh without serious injury?

(This is to be obeyed when one is not in danger and in light of the law of love.)

Prayer

"Father, I place my marriage in Your perfect hands. Give me new eyes to see my spouse. Help me be kind. You are able to meet my needs, so I look to what I can give to the one I love."

Jesus' Words that Point to this Commandment

Matthew 5:31-32, Matthew 19:4-9, Mark 10: 2-12, Luke 16:18

> *Jesus said,*
> *"It is wrong for you to divorce your wife so that you can marry another-that is adultery. And when you take that one you have lusted after as a wife, and contribute to the breakup of her marriage, you are once again guilty of adultery." Luke 16:18 TPT*

How can I apply this to my life?

____

____

____

____

____

____

____

Be a Person of Your Word.

Red Letters

Jesus said, "Let your Yes be simply Yes, and your No be simply No; anything more than that comes from the evil one."
Matthew 5:37

Character and integrity are the result of a heart that is established in truth. Jesus is the way, the truth and the life. When we have a heart that follows Jesus, we desire honesty, integrity and truth.

Jesus is telling us to be a person of our word and a person of integrity. In 1 Chronicles 29:17 it says, "I know, my God, that You examine our hearts and rejoice when You find integrity there."

What is integrity?
Jesus tells you not to swear your promises - just say yes or just say no and follow through with them (Matthew 5:37). This is integrity.
Integrity is being on time. It is telling the truth. You show integrity when you return what isn't yours to take. Integrity stands up for a friend even when it costs something. A person of integrity only gives a promise that they can fulfill.

Your words and promises should be trusted. Sometimes our feelings change but when we give our word, it should not change.

In a court of law, a person who shows truth and integrity proves to be the strongest witness. Jesus needs you to be a strong witness. Walk in truth.

1 John 2:5 says when we follow through with our promises, the love of God is perfected in us. *Perfected.*

God always keeps His word to us.

Prayer

"Lord, help me be a person of integrity. Your Name and Your Word are one. You are trustworthy. My name and my word, likewise, are one. I receive Your wisdom when I choose to say "Yes" to something. Jesus, because You live in me, I am able to be a man/woman of excellence and can be called trustworthy."

Jesus' Words that Point to this Commandment

Matthew 5:33-37, Luke 6:31, John 5:19, John 14:6

> *"But whoever habitually keeps His word and obeys His precepts [and treasures His message in its entirety], in him the love of God has truly been perfected [it is completed and has reached maturity]. By this we know [for certain] that we are in Him: whoever says he lives in Christ [that is, whoever says he has accepted Him as God and Savior] ought [as a moral obligation] to walk and conduct himself just as He walked and conducted Himself. 1 John 2:5-6 AMP*

How can I apply this to my life?

____

____

____

____

____

____

____

____

Don't Hit Back.

Red Letters

Jesus said, "Here's another old saying that deserves a second look: 'Eye for eye, tooth for tooth.' Is that going to get us anywhere? Here's what I propose: 'Don't hit back at all.' If someone strikes you, stand there and take it. If someone drags you into court and sues for the shirt off your back, gift wrap your best coat and make a present of it. And if someone takes unfair advantage of you, use the occasion to practice the servant life. No more tit-for-tat stuff. Live generously."

Matthew 5:39 MSG

You are called to a higher way of living. You have been given a new life that is above the carnal way of man. You no longer need to personally bring justice to other people's actions.

There now dwells in you a love that is powerful enough to meet all your needs. You are called to habitually defer to that love. There is no threat, and no enemy able to take that from you.
You can serve humanity by this love even when life gets ugly.

The God of creation is defending you. He will bring perfect justice. Filled with this confidence, we follow Jesus and joyfully take the crown of humility He gives us.

When someone strikes you with an evil word, accusation, or even their fist, wait. Do not react quickly. Do not return the evil, but rather separate yourself. Remove yourself from the toxic anger so you can begin to yield to a supernatural love.

When someone steals from you, pray and listen. Jesus is the Lord of your life, not your emotions and neither is your pride.

Focus on Jesus. Be like Jesus. People expect you to fight back. React with compassion and surprise them all.
(Remember, Jesus' anger was never personal.)

You no longer only have carnal resources, now you have the riches of Heaven (and the armies of Heaven!) through Christ Jesus your Lord.

Prayer

"Lord, I humble myself before you and in Your perfect time you will exalt me. I lay down this problem and wait for Your wisdom. I lay down the need to control the outcome. Fill me to overflowing with Your love."

Jesus' Words that Point to this Commandment

Matthew 5:38-48, Matthew 18:1-5, Matthew 20: 27-28, Matthew 22:37-40, Mark 10:42-45, Mark 12:30-31, Luke 6:27-36, John 3:16, John 13:3-5, John 13:34-35, John 14:23

> *"You've observed how godless rulers throw their weight around," Jesus said, "and when people get a little power how quickly it goes to their heads. It's not going to be that way with you. Whoever wants to be great must become a servant. Whoever wants to be first among you must be your slave. That is what the Son of Man has done: He came to serve, not to be served—and then to give away his life in exchange for many who are held hostage."*
> *Mark 10:44-45 MSG*

How can I apply this to my life?

Be Known as a Giver.

Red Letters

Jesus said, "Learn to generously share what you have with those who ask for help, and don't close your heart to the one who comes to borrow from you." Matthew 5:42 TPT

When you are a giver, you proclaim with your actions, "I am free from greed." You are also reflecting your Father's character; "For God so loved the world that He gave His only begotten Son, that whosoever believes in Him will not perish, but have everlasting life" (John 3:16).

What is in your hand right now? Your gifts to share are not limited to finances. Can you share your time? A moment to listen? Talents and abilities? Prayer? Extra resources? A smile?

In every opportunity to give your resources, seek God's direction. If He gives you direction to give or lend to a neighbor, don't be afraid. Joyfully do it. There are more blessings than you can imagine ready to be poured on you when you open your hand to others.

If someone asks to borrow something, let them borrow it. If they promise to return it but don't, let it go. Don't get tangled up in getting it back. It will open the door to division and the enemy's work.

God also assures us that in the law of seedtime and harvest you are guaranteed to be blessed. When you give it is the same as planting a seed. That seed will grow up into a greater amount than what you planted, and you will receive more than what you gave.

Prayer

"Father, I give you my heart. I resist any fear. Your perfect love cleanses me of all fear. I love to give because You love to give. Reveal who needs a gift from me today."

Jesus' Words that Point to this Commandment

Matthew 5:42, Matthew 6:3-4, Matthew 10:8, Matthew 14:16-21, Matthew 19:21, Mark 4:26-29, Mark 6:37-44, Mark 10:21, Mark 12:41-44, Luke 6:30-38, Luke 12:33-34, John 3:16, John 11:22

> *Jesus said, "Give, and it will be given to you. They will pour into your lap a good measure—pressed down, shaken together, and running over [with no space left for more]. For with the standard of measurement you use [when you do good to others], it will be measured to you in return."*
>
> *Luke 6:38 AMP*

How can I apply this to my life?

____

____

____

____

____

____

____

____

If we love God, we will do whatever he tells us to.
And he has told us from the very first to love each other.

2 John 1:6 TLB

Give Quietly.

Red Letters

Jesus said, "When you give a gift to a beggar, don't shout about it as the hypocrites do—blowing trumpets in the synagogues and streets to call attention to their acts of charity! I tell you in all earnestness, they have received all the reward they will ever get."
Matthew 6:2 TLB

Don't make a big production of your giving. Do it quietly.
When you do a kind act for someone, do it secretly. God knows.
If you go around broadcasting what a great thing you have done, you seek your own praise.

Let the praise be given to God. Let His name be lifted up in thanksgiving.
When you allow the honor to be given to God, people focus on God.
When people focus on God they are healed, saved and delivered. The Kingdom of God is increased, and God has used your hands.
There is no greater reason to give.

Giving should be your mode of operation and not a special occurrence.
Jesus even goes so far to say in Matthew 6:3, "Don't let your left hand know what your right hand is doing." (He knows you might hurt yourself patting yourself on the back with that left hand!)
A person in the habit of giving doesn't need to make a big deal of it because it is who they are and what they do.

Your giving has eternal consequences. The Holy Spirit speaks to us and says, "For God will give to each one in return for what he has done. For those living in constant (quiet) goodness and doing what pleases Him, seeking an unfading glory and honor and imperishable virtue, will experience eternal life. But those governed by selfishness and self-promotion (the loud giver), whose hearts are unresponsive to God's truth and would rather embrace unrighteousness, will experience the fullness of wrath" (Romans 2:6-8 TPT).

Prayer

"Father, thank you for providing every good and perfect gift. Thank you for using me as your messenger. I am so blessed to be used by You. I want You to have all the glory!"

Jesus' Words that Point to this Commandment

Matthew 6:1-4, Matthew 6:21, Matthew 10:42, Matthew 25:33-40, Mark 12:41-44, Luke 12:31-34, Luke 21:2-4

> *And whoever gives to one of these little ones [these who are humble in rank or influence] even a cup of cold water to drink because he is my disciple, truly I say to you, he will not lose his reward.*
> *Matthew 10:42 AMP*

How can I apply this to my life?

____

____

____

____

____

____

____

Place Your Hands on Those Who are Sick and Pray for Them.

Red Letters

Follow Me in This:

As the sun went down that evening, all the villagers who had any sick people in their homes, no matter what their diseases were, brought them to Jesus; and the touch of his hands healed every one!

Luke 4:40 TLB

Believer in Jesus Christ, this commandment is for you.
You do not need to be ordained or trained to pray for the sick.

Begin by following Jesus' example and always ask those who need healing, if they WANT to be healed. If they are believers, ask if they believe Jesus will heal them.
If they believe Jesus can heal them, place your hands on them, pray for their need in Jesus' name, and allow God to do the work.

Why do we need to lay our hands on them?
The laying on of hands is a sacred movement that was used in the days of the Temple. "This is the thing (laying on of hands) that God commanded you to do, that God's Presence may appear" (Leviticus 9:6).
They would lay their hands on the sacrifice, offering it to God, and their hands became holy vessels for the Presence of God. We declare the sacrifice of Jesus on the cross, lay our hands on the sick, and the Presence of Jehovah-rophe, our Healer, comes on the scene. It is powerful.

Don't be afraid of a lack of results. That is not your responsibility. Jesus declared you should follow Him in this. It is your responsibility to obey

Jesus and it is God's might and power that does the work instantly or over a period of time.

The Lord is the Healer and we are His instrument.
God loves people and wants to pour His healing through your hands.
Laying your hands on the sick allows Jesus to touch them, through you.

Prayer

"Jesus, when people asked You if You would heal them while You walked the earth, You never said no. The Pharisees were the only ones who said there should be a limit on Your healing. You also said that there would be greater works when You went to the Father. I am part of Your greater works. I am part of the body of Christ on the earth. Use my hands to heal this generation. I release all the care and obey You in this. I allow Your healing ministry to continue to flow through these hands."

Jesus' Words that Point to this Commandment

Matthew 8:14-15, Matthew 9:28-30, Matthew 14:14, Matthew 19:14-15, Mark 6:5-13, Mark 7:3-35, Mark 8:22-25, Mark 10:16, Mark 16:17-18, Luke 4:40, Luke 13:11-13

> *Jesus said, "(To) those who believe: In My name...they will lay hands on the sick, and they will recover."*
> *Mark 16:15-18 NKJV*

How can I apply this to my life?

____

____

____

____

Give Up Anything That is More Important Than God.

Red Letters

The young man said, "I've done all the commandments. What's left?" "If you want to give it all you've got," Jesus replied, "go sell your possessions; give everything to the poor. All your wealth will then be in heaven. Then come follow me." Matthew 19:20-21 MSG

The Old Testament commandments still hold strong: Don't commit adultery, don't murder, don't steal, don't lie, don't defraud, honor your father and mother, and love your neighbor.
But in addition to obeying these, Jesus commands us to take it to the next level.

Taking it to the next level means you have to address your heart condition toward God.

This is where the true follower of Christ is separated. Being a Christian has many benefits, but you must also be willing to "carry your cross." You must be willing to put to death what you take pride in and be ready to walk away from every tie to the world and that includes your possessions, your desires, your plans, and purposes.

Idols come in many ways. They are anything that you love in the deepest place in your heart and because of that love, you serve them.
If they were removed, would you, the real you, be left?
If you were asked to give it up, could you do it?

Jesus does not share the throne within your heart with anyone or anything. He said, "You cannot serve two masters. Either you will hate the one and love the other, or you will be devoted to one and despise the other" (Matthew 6:24 NIV).

Even dreams can be idols. Can you release them just as Jesus asked this wealthy young man, and follow Jesus? But when you come to that decision, get ready, because God will lead you to your true desires.

He is a good God. Surrender your heart to Him, He will care for it. "Never doubt God's mighty power to work in you and accomplish all this. He will achieve infinitely more than your greatest request, your most unbelievable dream, and exceed your wildest imagination! He will outdo them all, for His miraculous power constantly energizes you!" (Ephesians 3:20 TPT).

Prayer

"Lord, I surrender my life to You. Let Your plans be my plans. You formed me before I was born. You took pleasure in the gifts You placed in me. You know things about me that I have yet to discover. The plans You have for me are exciting. There is no one on the earth like me and that makes You smile. What would You have me do?"

Jesus' Words that Point to this Commandment

Matthew 4:1-11, Matthew 6:19-21, Matthew 7:13-14, Matthew 9:17, Matthew 16:24-27, Matthew 19:18, Mark 10:19-30, Luke 10:25-28

> *Then Jesus said to the disciples, "If anyone wants to be a follower of mine, let him deny himself and take up his cross and follow me."*
> *Matthew 16:24*

How can I apply this to my life?

____

____

____

____

Seek Heavenly Treasure, Not Earthly Wealth.

Red Letters

"Don't hoard treasure down here where it gets eaten by moths and corroded by rust or—worse!—stolen by burglars. Stockpile treasure in heaven, where it's safe from moth and rust and burglars. It's obvious, isn't it? The place where your treasure is, is the place you will most want to be, and end up being." Matthew 6:19-21 MSG

This commandment is about your focus.

Part of the blessing of Abraham you inherited when you accepted Jesus was earthly treasures. But if your focus is trying to get rich, you will find yourself reaching for an unattainable goal and exhausted in the process.

When a person's focus is on obtaining wealth, their mind is racing toward how to get there first, how to protect it, how to maintain it, and how to increase it. It is a never-ending balancing act that requires all of your focus and in the end, you leave it.

An investment that disappears at the point of death.

Jesus is actually giving investment advice that has a much bigger payoff. Our life on earth is placed in a box of time. There is another existence outside that box.

We have an opportunity to invest now in that existence.

And Jesus is advising us to invest in that heavenly treasure because it goes with us.

A heart that dwells on earthly treasure will end up empty. A heart that focuses on heavenly treasure will overflow for eternity.

You receive this heavenly treasure by meditating on God's Word. You build up storehouses of heavenly wealth by spending time in prayer at the feet of Jesus. In addition to an increase of wisdom and wellbeing you will get a heavenly perspective.

You will find this wealth will benefit your spirit, soul, and your body. You will bring hearts to Jesus when you overflow with this wealth. They will spend eternity in Heaven because you shared His wealth with them. And no one can take this from you.

Prayer

"Lord, I put my eyes on You. Like your disciple Mary, I will sit at Your feet, open my heart and hear Your voice. Pour Your perfect love into my heart. Fill me to overflowing. I will do what You have called me to do and you provide more than enough. I seek You first and all these wonderful things will follow."

Jesus' Words that Point to this Commandment

Matthew 6:19-24, Matthew 13:44-46, Matthew 16:15-19, Mark 8:33, Luke 12:16-34, Luke 16:19-31, John 4:34-36

> *"Yes, every man is a fool who gets rich on earth but not in heaven." Then turning to his disciples he said, "Don't worry about whether you have enough food to eat or clothes to wear. For life consists of far more than food and clothes." Luke 12:21-23 TLB*

How can I apply this to my life?

____

____

____

____

____

Forgive. Forgive. Forgive.

Red Letters

Jesus said, "And whenever you stand praying, if you have anything against anyone, forgive him and let it drop (leave it, let it go), in order that your Father Who is in heaven may also forgive you your [own] failings and shortcomings and let them drop. But if you do not forgive, neither will your Father in heaven forgive your failings and shortcomings." Mark 11:25-27 AMP

This is an important commandment and one that Jesus repeated in many teachings.

You are not releasing someone from their actions when you forgive, you are releasing yourself from being possessed by their actions.

Unforgiveness damages your heart. It affects your decisions, your ability to love others, your perspective, and your self-worth.

Forgiveness is like removing a thorn that has lodged in your foot. Any pressure on the thorn results in more agony and a reminder of the original injury, so you change your entire way of walking. The injury festers and infects your well-being. You can go back to the bush the thorn came from and burn it, but healing cannot begin until you remove the thorn.

Jesus is making it clear that forgiveness has less to do with the person who wronged you and more to do with your relationship with God Himself. When you hold a grudge against someone it damages your heart relationship with God because God is love. This is serious and probably why Jesus repeated the commandment to forgive so often.

Have faith in God and simply obey this command. Do not refuse to forgive, it only gives power to the enemy.

Forgive by faith. Say it aloud or even better write it down, declare it to heaven, and release the thorn to God.
When anger or another emotion rears its ugly head, and tries to convince you forgiveness never happened, you can respond with a reminder of the moment you decided to forgive. The thorn was released.

Your healed heart will be able to come boldly to your Heavenly Father and receive forgiveness and grace. And God will bring His perfect justice.

Prayer

"Lord, take any bitterness in my heart. I forgive those who have hurt me. Heal my emotions in this area. I make the decision right now to forgive__________. Whenever I think about the hurt, I ask You to renew my mind and I resist re-connecting myself to their actions."

Jesus' Words that Point to this Commandment

Matthew 6:14-15, Matthew 12:7, Matthew 18:21-35, Matthew 26:28, Mark 11:22-26, Luke 6:37, Luke 11:4, Luke 17:3-4, Luke 23:33-34, John 20:19-23

> *Then Peter came to him and asked, "Sir, how often should I forgive a brother who sins against me? Seven times?" "No!" Jesus replied, "seventy times seven!" Matthew 18:21-22 TLB*

How can I apply this to my life?

____

____

____

____

Be Diligent to Put a Guard Over Your Heart.

Red Letters

Jesus said, "A good man out of the good treasure of his heart brings forth good; an evil man out of the evil treasure of his heart brings forth evil. For out of the abundance of the heart the mouth speaks."
Luke 6:45 NKJV

Jesus is not referring to your physical heart. He is talking about the place where your mind and desires meet to choose good and evil. It is the center of your being: the resting place of your mind, will, and emotions.

The purpose and future of a person is found in their heart. This is where desires are grown. They spring up and flow out of the mouth. These words direct your life. Jesus is commanding you to guard your heart because your life depends on it.

There are two entrances to the heart that must be diligently guarded: the eye-gate and the ear-gate. What we chose to hear and see plant the seeds of our desires. The only way evil can enter the heart of person is when that person chooses to fill his eye-gate and ear-gate with evil and then give it an opportunity to take root.

Those evil thoughts soon grow into a desire and then find their way into a person's words, then they give birth to action. Murder, adultery, fornication, theft, covetousness, criticism, pride, and foolishness come from within and destroy a person's life. Choose what goes into your heart.

Plant what is good in your heart. The Word of God is 100% good and it will wash your heart clean. Let it take root. Read it, hear it, and say it. It will grow in there and produce beautiful fruit in your life.

What you see will be seen through the Word and what you hear will be heard through the Word. As it grows it will bring health to your mind, emotions, and body. Wisdom and well-being will dwell there.

You will know who you are and Who is your Source. His desires become your desires: you will desire truth and produce truth.
A well spring of life will flow to every area of your life.
Watch what you allow in your heart, your future depends on it.

Prayer
"Lord, You know my heart. I present it to You today for cleansing. Wash me clean. Purify my heart of any worldly desires I have let take root there. I need Your understanding and discernment in my heart. Today, I will allow Your Holy Spirit to guide me concerning what I allow in my ears and eyes. Help me guard my heart with all diligence."

Jesus' Words that Point to this Commandment

Matthew 5:27-28, Matthew 6:21-23, Matthew 11:28-29, Matthew 12:34-37, Matthew 13:15-23, Matthew 13:31-33, Matthew 15:8, Matthew 15:18-20, Matthew 22:37, Mark 7:20-23, Mark 12:30, Mark 16:14, Luke 6:45, Luke 8:12-15, Luke 21:34-36

> *Jesus said, "For their hearts are fat and heavy, and their ears are dull, and they have closed their eyes in sleep, so they won't see and hear and understand and turn to God again and let Me heal them. But blessed are your eyes, for they see; and your ears, for they hear. Many a prophet and godly man has longed to see what you have seen and hear what you have heard, but couldn't."*
> *Matthew 13:15-17 TLB*

How can I apply this to my life?

____

____

Fast Secretly.

> *Red Letters*
>
> *Jesus said, "But when you fast, perfume your head and wash your face, So that your fasting may not be noticed by men but by your Father, Who sees in secret; and your Father, Who sees in secret, will reward you in the open."*
>
> *Matthew 6:17-18 AMP*

If you believe that Jesus is Lord of your life, you have been born again of the Spirit of God. When this took place, your spirit was made perfect. Your spirit is fully healed. Your spirit hears God perfectly. Your spirit does not need to grow-it is who you will be for eternity.

Our daily challenge is getting our mind, will, emotions, and body in line with our spirit. Fasting creates this alignment.

Fasting will give your spirit power and quiet the voice of your flesh. The most common form of fasting is refraining from eating for a set period of time, but it is not limited to diet. You can fast anything that takes your focus off of Jesus. We fast from the things that "conform us to the world" (Romans 12:2).

As your flesh is quieted, make time to open your spiritual eyes and ears to the Holy Spirit. Set large amounts of time to pray and worship as you align your desires on Him. You will be able to hear God's voice more clearly. He has your answer and He is ready to share a new thing.

No one else needs to know you are fasting because it is an intimate act of communication between you and your God.

Your reward will be wisdom.

Prayer

"I will follow You Lord Jesus and separate myself from the authority of my appetite. I am a new creation, born of Your Spirit. I walk in the spirit. My soul (mind, will and emotions) helps me discern situations but I am not led by it. My body is useful for living on this earth and I care for it, but I am not led by my body. My spirit leads me. I am hungry for Your Word. I am thirsty for Your salvation. Guide me in this, Lord."

Jesus' Words that Point to this Commandment

Matthew 4:1-4, Matthew 6:16-18, Matthew 9:15, Matthew 17:20-21. Mark 9:25-29, Luke 5:35, Luke 18:1-14

> *And Jesus replied to them, "Can the guests of the bridegroom mourn while the bridegroom is with them? The days will come when the bridegroom is taken away from them, and then they will fast." Matthew 9:15 AMP*

How can I apply this to my life?

____

____

____

____

____

"Teacher, which is the greatest commandment in the Law?" Jesus replied: "Love the Lord your God with all your heart and with all your soul and with all your mind. This is the first and greatest commandment. And the second is like it: Love your neighbor as yourself. All the Law and the Prophets hang on these two commandments." Matthew 22:36, Luke 10:27, Mark 12:30-31

Do Not Let Your Eyes Be Filled with Evil Images.

Red Letters

"The light of the body is the eye: therefore, when thine eye is single, thy whole body also is full of light; but when thine eye is evil, thy body also is full of darkness."

Luke 11:34 KJV

Jesus is giving us another commandment on the importance of what we put our eyes on. Why? Because what you put your eyes on determines your focus.

Whatever you focus on, your thought life and actions will follow, and it becomes your goal.
Even in the natural life, if your eyes are focused on the ground, the head follows and leads the body in that direction. When a dancer spins, if their focus is down they will fall.

Fill your eye with fearful images, you will be fearful. Fill them with violence, you will be filled with violence. Fill them with sexual images, your thoughts will be filled with distorted sexuality.

The eye is the gateway and you are the gatekeeper. Don't take lightly what you watch. Evil images will fill your whole body and mind with darkness.

Watching worldly entertainment will dull your awareness of sin and its destruction. The enemy of our soul has used media as a powerful weapon to propagate many lies including one that says sexual immorality doesn't hurt you.
In truth, it is a blade that has left many hearts to bleed.

In Romans 13:12, the Holy Spirit instructs us to "cast off the works of darkness and put on the armor of light." Focus on God who is "Light and in Him is no darkness at all" (1 John 1:5).

As a matter of fact, He spoke, "Light be!" and that light is still unfolding at the borders of the universe. We are His children and He calls us "children of the light and children of the day. We do not belong to the night or to the darkness" (1 Thessalonians 5:5).

<u>Prayer</u>

"Lord, heal my eyes. Heal my heart from what I have seen. Wash my eyes and heart with the water of Your Word. Your Word covers them so everything I see and believe is filtered through Your Word."

<u>Jesus' Words that Point to this Commandment</u>

Matthew 6:22-23, Matthew 5:29, Matthew 18:9, Mark 9:47, Luke 11:34-36

> *"If your eye causes you to stumble and sin, throw it out [that is, remove yourself from the source of temptation]! It would be better for you to enter the Kingdom of God with one eye, than to have two eyes and be thrown into hell." Mark 9:47 AMP*

How can I apply this to my life?

____

____

____

____

____

____

____

Red Letters

Jesus said, "No servant is able to serve two masters; for either he will hate the one and love the other, or he will stand by and be devoted to the one and despise the other. You cannot serve God and mammon (riches, or anything in which you trust and on which you rely)."
Luke 16:13 AMP

Jesus said, "You shall worship the Lord your God, and Him only you shall serve" (Luke 4:8). Worship means to respect, revere, and call worthy someone or something.

Ask yourself these questions: What determines my schedule? What gets me out of bed in the morning? What is the deciding factor in my life? Who do I obey above all else? What do I spend my time on?
Your answers will point to what and whom you serve.

It is good to work. God worked by forming the earth and the heavens in six days and then rested. God created man to reflect Him and work with Him in the world. But we cannot let work become our source.

To help us understand this, we see an important interaction between Jesus and a young man in the gospels (Matthew 19:16-22). The scriptures tell us he was wealthy and in charge of ruling or managing a number of people. He was, in today's standards, a very successful businessman.

He takes a moment out of his busy schedule to hear Jesus. We see that he respects Jesus and recognizes His excellent teaching, but he also gives credit to his own spiritual success. He confidently trusts in himself. Jesus responds to his self-importance with, "If I am the wonderful Master you say I am, then walk away from everything you take confidence in and put your trust in Me." The young man couldn't. He had another master.

A follower of Jesus Christ follows Him seven days a week, not just on Sunday.

This commandment is not about money being evil, it is about who you truly serve. It is absolutely God's will for you to honor your responsibilities, but always be led by God. Let your life be a continuous prayer. Your character at work should reflect the One you serve.

Prayer

"Lord, I repent of placing anything above You. You alone are worthy. You have answered my prayers. You have given me Your best, even your own blood as a payment for my failures. You have never left me. You have provided for me and so much more. I will glorify You with my life."

Jesus' Words that Point to this Commandment

Matthew 4:10, Matthew 6: 24, Mark 10:24-31, Luke 16:10-15, John 4:24,34-38

> *The devil took Him to a very high mountain and showed Him all the kingdoms of the world and their splendor. "All this I will give you," he said, "if you will bow down and worship me." Jesus said to him, "Away from Me, Satan! For it is written: Worship the Lord your God, and serve Him only." Matthew 4:9-10 NIV*

How can I apply this to my life?

____

____

____

____

Do Not Stress About Your Life.

Red Letters

Jesus said, "If God gives such attention to the appearance of wildflowers—most of which are never even seen—don't you think he'll attend to you, take pride in you, do his best for you?
What I'm trying to do here is to get you to relax, to not be so preoccupied with getting, so you can respond to God's giving. People who don't know God and the way he works fuss over these things, but you know both God and how he works. Steep your life in God-reality, God-initiative, God-provisions. Don't worry about missing out. You'll find all your everyday human concerns will be met." Matthew 6:30-33 MSG

Stress is a human response to pressure. It can be present in the mind, the emotions, or the body. It manifests the moment when a problem bears down, and you have run out of resources (time, money, patience, physical strength etc.) to handle it.
Everyone (believers included) deals with stress. Jesus told us we would (John 16:33). Life on earth just seems to regularly provide stressful situations. <u>How</u> you react to these situations is what Jesus is addressing.

Your reaction is more important than you think. It determines what you really believe. A person who does not fully trust in God will lean on their own limited resources and understanding. The mind will turn solutions over and over until it exhausts itself.

As a believer, we turn to the words of Jesus. We make the life-giving decision to go to the Word of God and place all of our trust in His ability, not our own. His Holy Spirit instructs us, "Be anxious for nothing, but in everything by prayer and supplication (simply asking), with thanksgiving, let your requests be made known unto God; and the peace of God, which passes all understanding, will guard your hearts and minds through Christ Jesus" (Philippians 4:6) Jesus *promises* you peace.

Anxiety makes its home in the self-sufficient place inside our soul. If you are a true believer in El Shaddai-The All Sufficient God, it will have no place to settle. Take a deep breath. Go to the Word concerning your situation. Speak the Word over it. Take another deep breath and thank Him. You are not alone. His provision for you was put in place even before the problem arose.

Prayer

"Father, I know You love me. You have not put me in this tight place, but You have made a way for me to get out of it. I repent of any decision I made that put me here. I will not be afraid. I believe in my Savior Jesus Christ and His authority over this situation. I believe in every promise You have given me to provide my every need. Thank you for Your faithfulness and mercy."

Jesus' Words that Point to this Commandment

Matthew 6:25-34, Matthew 11:28-30, Matthew 13:22-23, Luke 6:48, Luke 8:14-15, Luke 12:22-34, Luke 21:19,34-36, John 14:26-27, John 16:33

> *"The seed which fell among the thorns, these are the ones who have heard, but as they go on their way they are suffocated with the anxieties and riches and pleasures of this life, and they bring no fruit to maturity. But as for that seed in the good soil, these are the ones who have heard the word with a good and noble heart, and hold on to it tightly, and bear fruit with patience." Luke 8:14-15*

How can I apply this to my life?

____

____

____

Ask God.

Red Letters

Jesus said, "Keep on asking and it will be given you; keep on seeking and you will find; keep on knocking [reverently] and [the door] will be opened to you." Matthew 7:7 AMP

How often do you encounter a problem in life and forget to ask God what to do?

I heard a clever phrase once, "Go to the throne, not the phone." (And this was before there was a "google" search on our phone.) Talking the problem with friends gives you some company, but rarely a solution. Many of us believe it was our mistakes that got us into a predicament, so it will be our responsibility to get ourselves out. Why do we go to the world first? The world is a chaotic mix of opposing opinions.

God is saying, "I have your solution. I am a good Father. Ask Me."
In every situation, ask God.
Be intimate in your relationship with God. Enter into the "secret place" where He waits to replace your weakness with His strength. He will replace the darkness with light. He will reveal the hidden things. His comfort is like no other.

God loves sharing in the details of your life. You were created for fellowship with your heavenly Father. Before the fall of man, Adam and Eve walked with God in the cool of the day. I imagine the Creator and His children sharing the events of the day and what they were planning for the next day. All the while enjoying one another's company.
We can now come face to face with God because of Jesus Christ. This was His redemption plan all along.

Jesus, our Savior, went to the top of the mountain to just spend time with His Father in prayer. When He walked down off that mountain, he walked on water. He is the God of the impossible and He will fill your imagination with new ideas and possibilities. He wants to hear from you regarding everything that is on your mind.

The only thing He requires is an atmosphere of faith; know that He is, know that He loves you, and know that He is able. Hebrew 11:6 says "Without faith no one can please God. Whoever comes to God must believe that he is real and that he rewards those who sincerely try to find him."

Prayer

"Lord, just like the author of Psalm 121, I know the help I need comes from You. You have made it all and You give me wisdom when I ask You for it. Help me in the big and small things. I love to spend time with You. Thank you for always giving me the solution."

Jesus' Words that Point to this Commandment

Matthew 7:7-11, Matthew 18:19, Matthew 21:22, Mark 11:24, Luke 11:5-13, John 11:22-26, John 14:13, John 15:5-7, John 15:16, John 16:24-28

> *"What father among you, if his son asks for a fish, will give him a snake instead of a fish? Or if he asks for an egg, will give him a scorpion? If you, then, being evil [that is, sinful by nature], know how to give good gifts to your children, how much more will your heavenly Father give the Holy Spirit to those who ask and continue to ask Him!" Luke 11:11-13 AMP*

How can I apply this to my life?

___

___

___

Don't Be Critical.

Red Letters

Jesus said, "Don't pick on people, jump on their failures, criticize their faults— unless, of course, you want the same treatment. That critical spirit has a way of boomeranging. It's easy to see a smudge on your neighbor's face and be oblivious to the ugly sneer on your own. Do you have the nerve to say, 'Let me wash your face for you,' when your own face is distorted by contempt? It's this whole traveling road-show mentality all over again, playing a holier-than-thou part instead of just living your part. Wipe that ugly sneer off your own face, and you might be fit to offer a washcloth to your neighbor." Matthew 7:1-2 MSG

You actually can't see a person's faults clearly until you remove your own. When all you see are the faults of others, it's your own faults that cloud your vision.

Jesus wants us to resist the temptation to pat ourselves on the back and set everyone else straight. He was without sin, died on the cross for us, rose from the dead with absolute victory, and now sits on the only throne that is worthy of perfect judgement.

James 4:12 says, "There is only one Lawgiver and Judge, the One who has power to save and destroy-so who do you think you are to judge your neighbors?" Jesus is that Judge and His response to our short-comings and failures is an outpouring of kindness and mercy when we come to Him.

Judging other begins with jealousy. We also read in the book of James (4:2), "You jealously want what others have so you begin to see yourselves better than others...and all the time you don't obtain what you want because you won't ask God for it!"

Instead of pointing the finger, straighten your walk with the Lord, obtain what you need from Him, and your life will inspire those around you to change.

Prayer

"Forgive me Lord for being quick to criticize. My job is to love those You have put in my life. It's Your love that has the power to change. Help me put my energy and focus toward changing my faults, not others."

Jesus' Words that Point to this Commandment

Matthew 7:1-5, Luke 6:37-45, John 8:3-11, John 17:1-2, John 21:20-22

> *Teacher," they said to Jesus, "this woman was caught in the very act of adultery. Moses' law says to kill her. What about it?" They were trying to trap him into saying something they could use against him, but Jesus stooped down and wrote in the dust with his finger. They kept demanding an answer, so he stood up again and said, "All right, hurl the stones at her until she dies. But only he who never sinned may throw the first!"*
>
> *John 8:4-7 TLB*

How can I apply this to my life?

____

____

____

____

____

Don't Share if They Don't Care.

Red Letters

Jesus said, "Do not give that which is holy (the sacred thing) to the dogs, and do not throw your pearls before hogs lest they trample upon them with their feet and turn and tear you in pieces." Matthew 7:6 AMP

Share the good news. Share what God has done for you as you are led by the Holy Spirit. Let your life be a continuous celebration of Jesus. You will be heard.

There will be times when the heart of the hearer will soften. Watch closely. When this happens, go deeper. Let His Truth unfold as you answer their questions.

There will also be times when the hearer's ear is closed. Like trying to water a rock, the gospel is met by resistance and debate. They push it away. Jesus' instructions are: your work there is done.
Don't keep beating them over the head with it. You could have planted a seed that might have found its way into a crack, and over time it may grow.

People are not saved by you. They are saved by Jesus.
Release yourself of the responsibility and let go.

Let God speak to them and joyfully move on.
Sometimes you are laying down a small portion of their path to the Lord.

Prayer

"Lord, give me courage to share the gospel everywhere I go. Teach me

how to be led by Your Holy Spirit. I am Your follower and You never entertained arguments over who You were. You walked through the angry crowd unscathed and kept Your focus on Your Heavenly Father. Help me do the same."

Jesus' Words that Point to this Commandment

Matthew 7:6, Matthew 10:7-14, Luke 9:5

> *"Then (Jesus) commissioned them to preach God's kingdom realm and to heal the sick to demonstrate that the kingdom had arrived. As He sent them out, He gave them these instructions: Take nothing extra on your journey. Just go as you are. Don't carry a staff, a backpack, food, money, not even a change of clothes. Whatever home welcomes you as a guest, remain there and make it your base of ministry. And wherever your ministry is rejected and not welcomed, you are to leave that town and shake the dust off your shoes as a testimony before them."*
>
> *Luke 9:2-5*

How can I apply this to my life?

____

____

____

____

____

Jesus said, "Whoever breaks one of these commandments, and teaches others to do so, he will be called least in the kingdom of heaven: but whoever will do and teach them, he will be called greatest in the kingdom of heaven." Matthew 5:19

Treat Others the Same Way You Want to Be Treated.

Red Letters

"And as you would like and desire that men would do to you,
do exactly so to them."
Luke 6:31 AMP

This is the golden rule of Christianity. It is the foundation of true justice. Master this and you will be walking in victorious kingdom of God living. It will bring order and peace to everything you do.

How would you like to be treated?

Take a few minutes and write down how you would like to be treated by your friends, family, and co-workers. Be specific.

Now make a list of what you can do to treat others this way.

Start today.

Jesus is calling you to be different than the world. It takes courage and strength to be different.
The unrestrained, personal love God has for you provides you with the courage and strength to return good for evil, blessings for curses.

Jesus said, "The greatest among you will be the one who always serves others from the heart. Remember this (*put your name here): If you have a lofty opinion of yourself and seek to be honored, you will be humbled. But if you have a modest opinion of yourself and choose to humble yourself, you will be honored" (Matthew 23:11-12 TPT).

This is the way the kingdom of God works here on earth.

Prayer

"Jesus, I want to see with Your eyes. I put on the cross all of my self-centered goals and prideful thoughts. Thank you for laying Your love across my shoulders. I will love others as You love me."

Jesus' Words that Point to this Commandment

Matthew 7:12, Matthew 22:37-40, Mark 12:29-31, Luke 6:31-36, Luke 10:25-37

> *Jesus said, "And the second is like, namely this,*
> *Thou shalt love thy neighbor as thyself.*
> *There is none other commandment greater than these."*
> *Mark 12:31 KJV*

How can I apply this to my life?

____

____

____

____

____

____

____

He has shown you, O mortal, what is good. And what does the Lord require of you? To act justly and to love mercy and to walk humbly with your God. Micah 6:8

Choose Your Spiritual Leaders Wisely.

Red Letters

"Beware of false prophets, who come to you dressed as sheep, but inside they are devouring wolves. You will fully recognize them by their fruits. Do people pick grapes from thorns, or figs from thistles? Even so, every healthy (sound) tree bears good fruit worthy of admiration, but the sickly (decaying, worthless) tree bears bad worthless fruit."

Matthew 7:15-17 AMP

Be wise. When you choose to follow a spiritual leader don't get caught up in the excitement. Look around and see who else is following. Look around at the fruit of their ministry. Listen closely to what they are saying.

First of all, their ministry should acknowledge Jesus as the Son of God and the Bible as the written Word of God. They should acknowledge the Holy Spirit, given by Jesus. They should be sensitive to His presence and ready to receive His guidance. There should be people who are growing in knowledge of the Word through their ministry.

Beware of a church leader that has bad results from their work.
Do not follow a wicked man that appears holy. Beware of a leader that stirs up division and strife with other Christians. Beware of a leader with unholy conduct. Beware of a leader that teaches good principles of living but does not bring sinners to God for repentance and cleansing through Jesus Christ.

These people are dangerous to your soul.

Prayer

"Lord, I seek Your wisdom. I lay at Your throne any worldly lusts that draw me to the wrong leadership. Thank you for guiding me to leaders who are like You; good shepherds who guide, protect and feed their flock with Your holy Word."

Jesus' Words that Point to this Commandment

Matthew 7:15-23, Matthew 11:19, Matthew 21:12-14, Matthew 23, Matthew 24:11,24, Mark 13:21-22, Luke 12:1-3

By this time the crowd, unwieldy and stepping on each other's toes, numbered into the thousands. But Jesus' primary concern was his disciples. He said to them, "Watch yourselves carefully so you don't get contaminated with Pharisee yeast, Pharisee phoniness. You can't keep your true self hidden forever; before long you'll be exposed. You can't hide behind a religious mask forever; sooner or later the mask will slip and your true face will be known. You can't whisper one thing in private and preach the opposite in public; the day's coming when those whispers will be repeated all over town."
Luke 12:1 MSG

How can I apply this to my life?

____

____

____

____

____

Then [in the final time] I will give you [spiritual] shepherds after My own heart, who will feed you with knowledge and [true] understanding.
Jeremiah 3:15 AMP

Look to the Truth, Jesus.

Red Letters

Jesus said to him," I am the Way and the Truth and the Life; no one comes to the Father except by (through) Me." John 14:6 AMP

We live in a world that is littered with arrows that say, "This is the truth!" Every day we find ourselves buried in the white noise of politicians, musicians, authors, commentators, celebrities, commercials, etc. all sharing "the truth". It is an inherent human need to know who and what is true. We hunger for truth.

Jesus says, "Are you searching for the truth? Follow me. I am the way to Truth. It is a narrow path. Keep your eyes on Me. I am the beginning, the middle and the end."

Every day you need to look to the Truth, your Savior, Jesus Christ.

But how? Jesus sits in heaven and here we stand on earth. How do we look into His eyes? We read the Living Word, the Bible. This is how we see Him; through His Word.

What Jesus says can be trusted. Who He says you are, is who you are. If He says you are free, you are free. Where He says you are going, you are going.

His Truth will separate you from the chaos and confusion of the world. His Word is like a sword separating you toward the Truth and exposing the lies.

It is time to question what you have determined as the truth. What do you believe about yourself? What do you believe about the character of God? Is it true according to the Word of God? It is time to find out.

Prayer

"Jesus, I look to You for every answer. I hear Your voice when I am still. You are Lord of my life. There is no other way but by You. There is no other Truth on earth apart from You. My life is covered with Your life."

Jesus' Words that Point to this Commandment

Matthew 7:13-14, Matthew 11:5-6, Matthew 14:29 (Peter looks to Jesus), Mark 12:10, Luke 13:24, John 1:14-17, John 3:20-21, John 3:33, John 4:24, John 8:31-32, John 14:6-7, John 16:13, John 17:17, John 18:37-38

> *Jesus said, "Sanctify them through thy truth: thy word is truth."*
> *John 17:17 KJV*

How can I apply this to my life?

____

____

____

____

____

____

____

____

Jesus says, "Blessed are your eyes for they see and your ears, for they hear." Matthew 13:16

Give Glory and Thanks to God.

Red Letters

And one of them, when he saw that he was healed, turned back, and with a loud voice glorified God and fell down on his face at his feet, giving him thanks: and he was a Samaritan. So, Jesus answered and said, "Were there not ten cleansed? but where are the nine? Were there not any found who returned to give glory to God except this foreigner? And He said to him, "Arise, go your way. Your faith has made you well."

Luke 17:16-18 NKJV

Take this moment to thank God for what He has done for you.
Let time fold for a minute and thank Him for what He is going to do in your life.
Thank Him for His wonderful works that are unknown and unseen.

God is mighty in power and able to do great things. In the deafening power of thunder, lightning, and the crash of the seas, we only see a tiny glimpse of His power! His dominion is over all the earth and the heavens. He is THE highest authority and He cares about you.

God will answer your prayer and when He does, give Him thanks and let all who hear of your answered prayer know He is faithful. Give Him the glory! Never be tempted to explain away a miracle.
Your thankful heart will open your life to even greater blessings. He will make you whole...just like the healed man in the above scripture.

What does it mean to give glory to God? It means we acknowledge Him to be who He says He is. It means we celebrate what he has done in our lives for all to see. It means we give the credit to Him.

Giving God the glory means we lean on His ability and power. We acknowledge that He is always faithful and we, daily, speak our "Amen" to all of these things.

Jesus was always in the habit of thanking God. He thanked Him before He saw a miracle, when He was witnessing a miracle, and after God moved on His behalf. This is our example.

Prayer

"Thank you, Lord, for Your faithfulness. Thank you for Your Son, Jesus! I believe all of Your promises find their fulfillment in Him. I choose to say 'Amen' to the promise that He is my Healer, my Redeemer, and my Deliverer. Thank you, Jesus! Thank you for all You have done for me and all You are going to do."

Jesus' Words that Point to this Commandment

Matthew 11:25-30, Matthew 15:36, Matthew 26:26-28, Mark 8:6-8, Mark 14:22-23, Luke 10:21, Luke 17:12-19, Luke 22:17-19, Luke 24:30-31, John 6:11, John 11:41

> *And (Jesus) took the seven loaves and the fishes, AND GAVE THANKS, and brake them, and gave to his disciples, and the disciples to the multitude. And they did all eat and were filled.*
> *Matthew 15:36-38 KJV*

How can I apply this to my life?

____

____

____

____

____

Cheer Up!

Red Letters

"I have told you these things, that My joy and delight may be in you, and that your joy and gladness may be of full measure and complete and overflowing." John 15:11 AMP

Jesus commands you to smile!
Your countenance will testify you know Jesus.

But what about those who are dealing with depressing circumstances?

In the gospels we are told of a man who is being brought in to Jesus by his family and friends. He is on a stretcher and in bad shape.
He needs healing and he needs it now. His situation is oppressing him to the point where he can't do anything for himself. Others feed him, dress him, and provide for him. Not only is his body weak, but his soul is tired and separated from any joy.

Jesus looks at the man and says, "Cheer up!"

You can imagine the puzzled look on the man's face. "Umm, I need to walk, they said you could help with that." Jesus just smiles at him and the man locks eyes with Jesus. The joy and delight in Jesus' eyes fill the heart of that man. The forgiveness and freedom of God flood his soul. He locks into that gift of joy.

Jesus knew, by faith, that diseased man would walk out whole, but healing always begins in the inner man. His command to him *and us* is, "Receive the joy before you receive the miracle!"

The Holy Spirit reaffirms this commandment in 1 Thessalonians 5:16, "Let joy be your continual feast (TPT)." This means to be joyous in every season. But how?

When we understand that joy is a gift given to us through the Holy Spirit, not an emotion, we can be the ones who make the choice to receive joy. Then we choose to walk in joy no matter what we see. We choose to look at the source of our joy, our Savior, Jesus. This choice will strengthen your inner man and put you in position to receive even more wonderful gifts from your Heavenly Father.

Prayer

"Lord, fill me with Your joy today. I will close my eyes and receive Your joy-filled embrace. I receive Your gift of joy. I declare aloud, in the name of Jesus, 'Get behind me oppression!' Lord, You have forgiven me and healed me. This smile is for You!"

Jesus' Words that Point to this Commandment

Matthew 5:11-12, Matthew 9:2, Matthew 25:21, Luke 2:10, Luke 6:22-23, John 15:10-11, John 16:22-24, John 17:13

> *Soon some men brought him a paralyzed man on a mat. When Jesus saw their faith, he said to the sick man, "Cheer up, son! For I have forgiven your sins!" Matthew 9:2 TLB*

How can I apply this to my life?

____

____

____

____

____

Get Up. Be Set Free from What Holds You Down.

Red Letters

"I say to you, arise, pick up and carry your sleeping pad or mat, and be going on home." Mark 2:11 AMP

Jesus wants you to live by faith in Him and His Word. If your circumstances are weighing you down and joy has left the building, it's time to shake off the dust and go where God is telling you to go.

Make a line in the sand and prepare to cross over. On one side, the negative reports and the weight of the cares of this world are like quicksand. On the other, the Rock of our Salvation is solid ground. This is where the promises of God come to pass by faith. It is the place where your life reflects the fullness of God.

Get up and cross over into the "promised" land.
When you are there, speak only His promises over your life: "I will live, and I will not die." "I am more than a conqueror through Him who loves me." "I have the wisdom of God" etc. Your words will secure your stance.

When you have crossed this line, the storms of life may come against you. Do not move. Don't change your beliefs. As long as your feet stay on His solid foundation you will not be destroyed.

When you have crossed, remind yourself you now wear a new garment. Don't put on the old one. Your new garment is made of praise (Isaiah 61:3). Praise crushes the despair you once wore.

Instead of the ground shifting, you will see your circumstances shifting. You will see the solid promises of God come to pass in your life.

But if you want to stay in this position of victory and leave behind a life of defeat, you must be diligent to remove all doubt (Mark 11:23). Choose to believe the Word of God above all else.

Prayer

"Lord, take these burdens. Take the heavy responsibilities and cares of this life. Take the condemnation. Take the guilt. Take the disappointments. Take the fear. I make a stand today and believe Your Word that says You have lifted me out of the slimy pit and set my feet on solid ground (Psalm 40). I will speak your promises not the problems from here on and I look forward to Your salvation in every area of my life."

Jesus' Words that Point to this Commandment

Matthew 9:2-8, Mark 2:11, Mark 5:41, Luke 5:24, Luke 7:14-15, John 5:5-9

> *Jesus said, "Everyone who hears my teaching and applies it to his life can be compared to a wise man who built his house on an unshakable foundation. When the rains fell and the flood came, with fierce winds beating upon his house, it stood firm because of its strong foundation." Matthew 7:24-27 TPT*

How can I apply this to my life?

Be Teachable.

Red Letters

"But new wine must be put into new bottles; and both are preserved."

Luke 5:38 KJV

Jesus is saying to you, "Be made new every day with a clean heart, so you can hold new revelations given by Me." God has something new for you to learn today. Don't rely on old revelations to carry you through a new day.

Begin by asking forgiveness and releasing your forgiveness toward those who have hurt you. This will create a blank page in your heart. It creates a fresh wind over your soul and your eyes and ears will be open to wisdom and insight. The Word will open the door to wide places of understanding.

Read a portion of the Bible every day. Be filled with a new supply of understanding of who God is and who you are. These new revelations will be like a road map you can follow to navigate God's kingdom: a new road every day.

Jesus is your good shepherd. He is the One who navigates those paths of righteousness for you (Psalm 23). He will speak, and you will hear (John 10:27). If He leads you beside a quiet brook of bliss or to the side of a high, uncharted mountain, you must remain teachable. To be taught, you must focus and be still.

God spoke through the prophet Isaiah these profound words, "Behold, I am doing a new thing; now it springs forth, do you not perceive it? I will make a way in the wilderness and rivers in the desert" (Isaiah43:19).

We do not want to be caught not paying attention when God is teaching us. He is doing a new thing right now and it is for your benefit.

Just as a child continues to grow every day in the natural world, we grow up in the knowledge of Christ every day.

Prayer

"Lord, fill me with Your knowledge. Your Word is bread to my spirit and good wine to my soul. The more I receive the more I can give. I ask for Your forgiveness and release my forgiveness. I humble myself today and receive your instruction."

Jesus' Words that Point to this Commandment

Matthew 9:17, Luke 5:36-39, Mark 2:22, Matthew 26:27-28, John 15:3

> *All Scripture is breathed out by God and profitable for teaching, for reproof, for correction, and for training in righteousness.*
> *2 Timothy 3:16 ESV*

How can I apply this to my life?

____

____

____

____

____

____

____

His [Jesus'] mother said to the servants, "Whatever He says to you, do it." John 2:5

Be Brave, by Faith.

Red Letters

But Jesus turning and seeing her said, "Take courage, daughter; your [personal trust and confident] faith [in Me] has made you well." And at once the woman was [completely] healed. Matthew 9:22 AMP

If Jesus were to personally come to you and place his hands on your shoulders, look you in the eye and say, "Stop being afraid. I have heard you. You have believed that I am your Deliverer, and that I am faithful to hear and answer your prayers. I am answering that prayer right now." What would you do? You would breathe a sigh of relief, smile and say thank you.

He loves you and is speaking this to you right now.

Your faith is the conductor for the power of God to touch you.
Do not waiver. Do not be afraid.

It does not take any courage to crumble under your circumstance and agree with a bad report. Not one of the people mentioned in the Hall of Faith, found in Hebrews 11, gave in to their evil report. If they stood against the storm, you can too.

Be brave, reach out, and receive boldly. Jesus will be pleased with you just as He was with the woman with the issue of blood in Matthew 9. She believed if she just reached out and touched His garment, she would be made whole.

If the will of God is to give you an abundant life, do not wait around for that life to just happen. This woman would have never received healing if she had waited for Jesus to find her. Our job is to step out boldly in faith.

Prayer

"Lord, I boldly come to Your throne of grace when I am in trouble. I release my own ability. Help me find the promises You give in your Word concerning my victory. I believe Your Word. My faith stance pleases You, so I will boldly say right now, 'If I touch You (You are Your Word), I will be made whole."

Jesus' Words that Point to this Commandment

Matthew 9:22, Matthew 8:13, Matthew 15:28, Matthew 8:7-10, Matthew 17:20, Matthew 21:21-22, Luke 7:50, Luke 8:48, Luke 17:19, Luke 18:42, Luke 7:2-9, Luke 12:27-31, Luke 17:6, Mark 5:34-42, Mark 10:52, John 4:49-53, John 5:24

And Jesus said to him, "All right, it's done. Your faith has healed you." And instantly the blind man could see and followed Jesus down the road!
Mark 10:52 TLB

How can I apply this to my life?

____

____

____

____

____

____

____

I Send You Out with This Charge:
***Pray** for laborers to do the work of the gospel.*
***Preach** the Kingdom of God: God's salvation through Jesus.*
***Heal** the sick.*
***Cleanse** the diseased.*
***Cast out** devils...do all of these in My Name.*

Red Letters

"Don't begin by traveling to some far-off place to convert unbelievers. And don't try to be dramatic by tackling some public enemy. Go to the lost, confused people right here in the neighborhood. Tell them that the kingdom is here. Bring health to the sick. Raise the dead. Touch the untouchables. Kick out the demons. You have been treated generously, so live generously." Matthew 10:7-8 MSG

Salvation is free.
His abundant life is free.
His forgiveness is free.
Eternal life is free.
You have been given freely, now you freely give.

It's time.

<u>Prayer</u>

"Lord, I will obey this commandment. I will pray because You prayed for me. I will preach with words and without words as I follow You. I will offer prayers for healing in the name of Jesus because Your mercy lives in me. I will stand in the authority You gave me by casting out unclean spirits with Your name. I will serve my fellow man.
Where would You have me go today?"

Jesus' Words that Point to this Commandment

Matthew 9:38, Matthew 10:1, 7-16, Matthew 28:16-20, Mark 16:15-18, Luke 10:2-17, John 14:12-14

> *Jesus went back into the region of Galilee and preached the wonderful gospel of God's kingdom realm. His message was this: "At last the fulfillment of the age is come!*
> *It is time for the realm of God's kingdom to be experienced in its fullness! Turn your lives back to God and put your trust in the hope-filled gospel!" Mark 1:14-15 TPT*

How can I apply this to my life?

____

____

____

____

____

____

____

____

____

____

We can be sure that we've truly come to live in intimacy with God, not just by saying, "I am intimate with God," but by walking in the footsteps of Jesus. 1 John 2:6 TPT

When You Share the Good News, Don't Overly Plan It.

Red Letters

Jesus said, "...And don't worry about what you'll say or how you'll say it. The right words will be there; the Spirit of your Father will supply the words." Matthew 10:20 MSG

You are fully equipped to share the gospel.
You do not need to memorize a speech or prepare an argument.
Simply be prepared to tell others your story.

You wear the armor of God: the helmet of salvation covers your head, the breastplate of righteousness covers your heart, and the belt of truth circles your core with strength. The shield of faith covers you from the attacks of the enemy. You hold the sword of the Spirit, which is God's powerful Word. And finally, for the purpose of this commandment, your feet are covered with protection to walk in wisdom and safety to share the gospel of peace. (Ephesians 6:10-18)

Let the love of God pour into your heart and let every approach be in kindness. You have the Holy Spirit guiding you with the perfect way to communicate with the listener.

Trust in Him. Sharing the gospel doesn't require anything but your time and will. Sometimes it's just a matter of slowing down, taking a deep breath, and being aware of the love of God in that moment. You will be able to hear His voice when you quiet your own. Listen more.

Prayer

"Lord, put into place divine appointments for me today. Give me Your wisdom on what to say. Give me a fresh supply of patience to hear the

heart cry of that person. Give me discernment on what You would have me do. Will I plant a seed, water the seed, or bring this person to You through the prayer of salvation? Father, supply the words."

Jesus' Words that Point to this Commandment

Matthew 10: 9-14, Matthew 10:19-20, Matthew 28:19, Mark 16:15-18, Luke 12:11-12

> *Jesus said, "Don't worry about defending yourself or be concerned about how to answer their accusations.*
> *Simply be confident*
> *and allow the Spirit of Wisdom access to your heart,*
> *and He will reveal in that very moment what you are to say to them." Luke 12:11 TPT*

How can I apply this to my life?

____

____

____

____

____

____

____

____

Every one of the Lord's commands is right; following them brings cheer. Nothing He says ever needs to be changed. The rarest treasures of life are found in His truth. Psalm 19:9-10 TPT

Don't Release Your Peace When People Oppose Your Beliefs.

Red Letters

Jesus said, "If you're not welcomed, not listened to, quietly withdraw. Don't make a scene. Shrug your shoulders and be on your way."
Mark 6:11 MSG

Jesus is telling you to not take it personally when you share the gospel with someone, and they reject it. Just move on and keep your peace. Your job is not to prove you are right in what you believe.

There is a war between light and darkness and Jesus, the Light of the world, has already won. When you share the good news and people reject that message, they are rejecting Jesus. This reaction is actually so much bigger than you (Luke 21:17).

Offense is a weapon of the enemy. Walk away from it.
Your job is to show the door to everlasting life: Jesus.

Let them walk through if they choose. His light will draw them in.
Never release your peace.

Remember this: "There is such a great peace and well-being that comes to the lovers of Your Word, and they will never be offended" (Psalm 119:116 TPT).

Prayer

"Lord, Your peace is a powerful covering over my mind and heart. I will not release it. Give me Your perspective. You do not get offended, so I won't. Help me to leave my work in Your hands."

Jesus' Words that Point to this Commandment

Matthew 10:13-14, Mark 6:11, Luke 9:5, John 14:26-27, John 15:18-20

> *My work was to plant the seed in your hearts, and Apollos' work was to water it, but it was God, not we, who made the garden grow in your hearts. The person who does the planting or watering isn't very important, but God is important because he is the one who makes things grow.*
>
> *1 Corinthians 3:6-7 TLB*

How can I apply this to my life?

____

____

____

____

____

____

____

____

____

Happy [blessed, considered fortunate, to be admired]
is the man who finds [skillful and godly] wisdom,
And the man who gains understanding and insight [learning from God's word and life's experiences], For wisdom's profit is better than the profit of silver, and her gain is better than fine gold.
Proverbs 3:13-14 AMP

Be Wise as a Serpent and Gentle as a Dove.

Red Letters

Jesus said, "Behold, I am sending you out like sheep in the midst of wolves; be wary and wise as serpents, and be innocent (harmless, guileless, and without falsity) as doves."
Matthew 10: 16 AMP

It is not the will of God to have His children be walked on by the world.

The miraculous and mighty power that raised Christ from the dead, now dwells in you (Romans 8:11). Take a moment and breathe that reality in. The more you yield to God's love, the more that power has place in your life.

With that power comes access to the Spirit of Wisdom, *and* the Spirit of Revelation (Ephesians 1:17). You have access to God's wisdom in every circumstance. His wisdom will bring a heavy anointing and break off any heavy thing the enemy would try to put on you.
With revelation knowledge comes confidence that nothing can harm you because you are indeed a child of God Almighty.

Keep your heart clean and you will clearly hear the voice of your Shepherd guiding you in things beyond your comprehension.

The power you receive will not puff you up. But instead, it will lead you to a life of kindness and compassion.

You will have the wisdom of a clever serpent and the gentleness of an innocent dove. His love makes you perfect and as Jesus is, so are you in this world (1 John 4:17).

Prayer

"Lord, everywhere I go today You go with me. Show me the subtle schemes of my enemy to try and drag me into sin and destroy my life. Sharpen my spiritual senses and at the same time, soften my heart toward the lost and hurting."

Jesus' Words that Point to this Commandment

Matthew 10:16, Luke 10:3, Luke 21:15

> *Jesus said, "Simply speak with the words of wisdom that I will give you...and none of your persecutors will be able to withstand the grace and wisdom that comes from your mouths." Luke 21:15 TPT*

How can I apply this to my life?

____

____

____

____

____

____

I love each of you with the same love that the Father loves Me. You must continually let My love nourish your hearts. If you keep my commands, you will live in my love, just as I have kept My Father's commands, for I continually live nourished and empowered by His love. My purpose for telling you these things is so that the joy that I experience will fill your hearts with overflowing gladness! -Jesus, John 15:9-11 TPT

Speak Up! Don't Be Quiet About What You Believe.

Red Letters

Jesus said, "Don't be intimidated.
Eventually everything is going to be out in the open, and everyone will know how things really are. So, don't hesitate to go public now."
Matthew 10:27 MSG

In the end, every knee will bow to the Lordship of Jesus and every tongue created will acknowledge He is the Son of God, even the ones who vehemently deny it now (Philippians 2:9-11).

In light of this absolute reality, Jesus is speaking to you right now:
"The things I have told you in darkness, you speak in the light and what I have told you privately, preach on the housetops!" (Matthew 10:27)

Don't be timid and hide under a worldly cloak.
As a child of God, it is not the garment that has been given to you.

When Jesus became your Savior, you were born into God's family.
The One who created it ALL lives in you and calls you His name! You are valuable to God. He has given you Jesus and through Him you have eternal life. Jesus makes His home in you and He is the light of the world.

Your very "being" is different. The Holy Spirit tells you in Ephesians 2:10 (TPT): "You are God's poetry, a re-created people. You will fulfill the destiny God has given you because you are joined to Jesus, the Anointed One. Even before you were born, God planned in advance your destiny and all the good works you would do to fulfill it!"

In light of this truth, when you enter a room the environment changes.

Do not let the world tell you to keep your ideas and beliefs to yourself.

Prayer

"Lord, I praise You for all you have done!! I will not be afraid. What could man do to me? Your Word is my authority. Thank you for reaching out and pulling me out of the mud of this world. You have placed me on Your Rock and I will give You the glory. All will know I am Yours."

Jesus' Words that Point to this Commandment

Matthew 4:13-17, Matthew 5:14-16, Matthew 10:27, Luke 11:35-36, John 8:12

Jesus said, "If you embrace the truth, it will release true freedom in your lives...If the Son sets you free from sin, then become a true son and be unquestionably free!" John 8:32,36 TPT

How can I apply this to my life?

____

____

____

____

____

____

And they overcame and conquered him (the accuser) because of the blood of the Lamb and because of the word of their testimony, for they did not love their life and renounce their faith even when faced with death. Revelation 12:11 AMP

Fear God, Not People.

Red Letters

Jesus said, "Don't be in fear of those who can kill only the body but not your soul. Fear only God, who is able to destroy both soul and body in hell." Matthew 10:28 TPT

Life preservation is a deep human instinct.
But Revelation 12:11 speaks of believers responding to the enemies of God this way: "And [the believers] have defeated [the enemy] by the blood of the Lamb and by their testimony. And they did not love their lives so much that they were afraid to die."

Jesus had to resist the temptation to preserve His own life rather than do the will of His Father. Because He did this, we enter into the greatest gift, eternal LIFE with Him.

Most of us will never be faced with giving our lives for Christ. But this choice will be found in our everyday decisions. Will you fear God, or will you fear people?
When Jesus says to fear God, He doesn't mean to be afraid. God is love and we know that there is no fear in love. We are to honor and respect His Presence and His Word in every moment.

Our time on earth is one hundred years at best.
Eternity is one hundred years a billion times over and more.
Don't worry about what people think of you. Don't stay quiet because people have told you to do so.
Do the will of God and you will really live.

Prayer

"Jesus, thank you that I am an overcomer because of the cross. Like Stephen in the book of Acts I will keep my eyes on You when the pressure is on. The things of this world are temporary but my life with You is forever. I will not cave in to the fear of man. Fill me with Your love and courage."

Jesus' Words that Point to this Commandment

Matthew 10:17-22, Matthew 10:28, Matthew 16:23, Luke 12:4-5

> *Jesus said, "When people realize it is the living God you are presenting and not some idol that makes them feel good, they are going to turn on you, even people in your own family. There is a great irony here: proclaiming so much love, experiencing so much hate! But don't quit. Don't cave in. It is all well worth it in the end."*
>
> *Matthew 10:22 MSG*

How can I apply this to my life?

____

____

____

____

____

____

____

For we are His workmanship, created in Christ Jesus for good works, which God prepared beforehand that we should walk in them.

Ephesians 2:10 KJV

Let Others Know You Are a Christian.

Red Letters

Jesus said, "Whosoever therefore shall confess me before men, him will I confess also before my Father which is in heaven."

Matthew 10:32 KJV

Being a friend of Jesus has the best benefits.
He has the most amazing Dad and calls you over to hang out anytime you want. He even calls you "family" and says what is His is yours.

Jesus always has your back even when you make bad decisions. He always answers when you call and will take you to places beyond what you could imagine.
He is the friend who chose your need when He went to the cross, not His own.

In return Jesus just asks you to let people know He is *your* friend.
Jesus says, "Let people know you are a friend of Mine and I will let God know you are a friend."

When that day comes, and you stand in judgement before the Father, Jesus will be at His right hand. Let the words that begin your eternity say, "Yes, this is a friend. And the people of his/her generation knew it."

Stand and be counted today with the victorious Savior who will return in power, surrounded by the awesome glory of God.
In that day you will be fortunate to be called His friend.

Prayer

"Lord, I am Yours. I am fully committed to You. Help me reflect Your glorious light. I do not want to fade into the darkness of the world. Bless me with Godly relationships who bring out the light of Christ in me."

Jesus' Words that Point to this Commandment

Matthew 10:32, Mark 8:38, Luke 9:26, Luke 12:8,9

Jesus said,
"When I, the Messiah, come in my glory and in the glory of the Father and the holy angels, I will be ashamed then of all who are ashamed of me and of my words now."
Luke 9:26 TLB

How can I apply this to my life?

____

____

____

____

____

____

____

____

____

There is a private place reserved for the lovers of God, where they sit near Him and receive the revelation-secrets of His promises. Psalm 25:14 TPT

Separate Yourself from the World and Its Ways.

Red Letters

Follow Me in This:

Jesus said, "Do not think that I have come to bring peace upon the earth; I have not come to bring peace, but a sword." Matthew 10:34 AMP

Your job is not to be at peace with the world. Your job is to share the peace that is in relationship with Jesus.

Jesus' truth separates the kingdom of God from the world's system. The borders of His kingdom are made with the Word of God.

The Holy Spirit tells us in Hebrews 4:12 that the Word of God is like a double-edged sword...dividing and discerning the thoughts and intentions of our hearts.

The heart is where Christians are separated from the world. And we do that by putting the Word of God IN our heart. Our will becomes formed by the Word. You have His truth in you, so *you* become separated.

"Choose this day whom you will serve" (Joshua 24:15), and you will keep choosing every day.

When you serve the kingdom of God you look different than the world; your countenance reflects your trust in God. You speak differently; your words contain blessings, not curses. You react differently; your love for people supersedes your pride. Your goals are different; success means you can give more and reach more people.

The world NEEDS you to be different. Your presence will alter their environment. Like salt, your testimony will preserve their lives.

Prayer

"Lord, purify me. Burn out all that is not of You. I am not conformed to this world. I am transformed by Your Word. I will learn of You, study Your ways, understand Your good plans for me and as a result I will be able to discern Your perfect will in my life. Help me be separated from the world in every respect. You have given me a new heart and a new spirit."

Jesus' Words that Point to this Commandment

Matthew 5:13-16, Matthew 10:34-38, Matthew 11:28-30, Matthew 13:15-16, Matthew 15:8-9, Matthew 16:24-27, Mark 9:50, Luke 12:51-53, Luke 14:26-35, Luke 18:18-30, John 17:22-23

Jesus said,

"You are the salt of the earth, but if salt has lost its taste (its strength, its quality), how can its saltness be restored? It is not good for anything any longer but to be thrown out and trodden underfoot by men. You are the light of the world. A city set on a hill cannot be hidden." Matthew 5:13 AMP

How can I apply this to my life?

Support Those Who Do Full-Time Ministry.

Red Letters

Jesus said, "If you welcome a prophet because he is a man of God, you will be given the same reward a prophet gets. And if you welcome good and godly men because of their godliness, you will be given a reward like theirs." Matthew 10:41 TLB

Support those who do the work of the gospel every day.
This means to open doors of opportunity for them, protect them, finance them, and pray for them.

We are one body. It takes all of us to accomplish God's work on the earth. When you financially support ministries and churches who are on the front lines of Christianity, you are vitally important to that organization. Their focus should never be finances.

The apostle Paul gave us more than seven books in New Testament. His words have instructed millions of believers, but he makes special mention of the givers in the Philippian church in this scripture: "You have so graciously provided for my essential needs during this season of difficulty. For I want you to know that the Philippian church was the only church that supported me in the beginning as I went out to preach the gospel. You were the only church that sowed into me financially...I mention this not because I am requesting a gift but that the fruit of your generosity may bring you an abundant reward" (Philippians 4:14-17 TPT).

If Paul had to support his own financial needs, we, the church, would not have had the full attention of his ministry, which we benefit from today.

Each member who contributed to Paul shared in his heavenly reward just by giving.
And here in this commandment Jesus promises that you too will share in the reward.

Prayer

"Lord, thank you for meeting all of my needs and the needs of Your faithful missionaries, pastors, and teachers. Reveal to me those who need my support. Let Your will be done here on earth as it is in Heaven. To You Father God, be glory forever and ever!"

Jesus' Words that Point to this Commandment

Matthew 10:40-42, Mark 9:41, Luke 6:38, Luke 12:33-34

Jesus said,
"If anyone so much as gives you a cup of water because you are Christ's— I say this solemnly—he won't lose his reward."
Mark 9:41 TLB

How can I apply this to my life?

____

____

____

____

____

Obey your spiritual leaders and recognize their authority, for they keep watch over your soul without resting since they will have to give an account to God for their work. So it will benefit you when you make their work a pleasure and not a heavy burden Hebrews 13:17 TPT

Do Not Doubt Me.

Red Letters

Jesus said, "And tell John that the blessing of heaven comes upon those who never lose their faith in Me-no matter what happens!"
Matthew 11:6 TPT

Resist the temptation to doubt.
You will have the opportunity through the twists and turns of life to doubt the sovereignty of Jesus because of bad circumstances.

Remember the storm in Matthew 14. The disciples were strong in faith and close followers of Jesus, but they got into trouble with that storm. Jesus showed up...but not to rescue them right away.
As He walked on the water, Jesus challenged Peter to take a step toward Him and do what looked impossible; not only walk on water but ignore the storm completely.
He told him to walk ON the storm.

When Peter locked eyes with Jesus and believed, he overcame any power that storm had to drag him down.

Jesus is saying to you right now, "Do not look at the storm that threatens you. Look at Me. Do not doubt in My ability or My promises."

The Holy Spirit reminds us of this commandment in James 4:7-8 (TPT), "Surrender to God. Stand up to the devil and resist him and he will turn and run away from you. Move your heart closer and closer to God, and He will come even closer to you. But make sure you cleanse your life...keep your hearts pure and stop doubting."

Prayer

"Lord, I do not doubt You. Your blessing is on me because You said to Thomas, 'Blessed are those who have not seen and yet have believed.' Thank you. The waves of my emotions do not determine my ability to trust You. My eyes are on You, my Savior, the author and finisher of my faith."

Jesus' Words that Point to this Commandment

Matthew 9:28-29, Matthew 11:3-6, Mark 5:36, Luke 7:23, John 20:29

> *But when you ask, you must believe and not doubt, because the one who doubts is like a wave of the sea, blown and tossed by the wind. That person should not expect to receive anything from the Lord. Such a person is double-minded and unstable in all they do.*
>
> *James 1:6-8 NIV*

How can I apply this to my life?

____

____

____

____

____

____

____

I will sing my song of joy to You, Yahweh, for in all of this you have strengthened my soul. My enemies say that I have no Savior, but I know I have one in You! Psalm 13:6 TPT

Beware of a False Security in Humanity.

Red Letters

Jesus said, ""The men of Nineveh shall arise against this nation at the judgment and condemn you. For when Jonah preached to them, they repented and turned to God from all their evil ways. And now one greater than Jonah is here—and you refuse to believe him."
Matthew 12:41 TLB

Don't be fooled into thinking you are safe in the world. Without God's salvation, there will be judgment and destruction greater than you have ever known.

The strongest lie of the antichrist spirit is that there is great power in the goodness of man.

Blockbuster movies end in the triumph of man's indomitable spirit. Man-made religions and self-help gurus stand on platforms that proclaim you are your best healer. They honor the god within, the power of the human will. They believe the future of the world, all humanity, lies in the hands of human intellect. It is the enemy's greatest lie.

Faith in humanity collapses into deadly chaos without the laws of a loving God.

Place your trust in the living God and His goodness.
Believe His Word, cling to His promises, and love people. He is a God of order.

When we submit our lives to Him, "the light of God illuminates the eyes of our imagination, flooding us with light, until we experience the full

revelation of the hope of His calling-that is the wealth of God's glorious inheritance that He finds in us" (Ephesians 1:16-19 TPT).
It is an amazing life knowing He is our security.

Prayer

"Lord, You are my God. I am your child. I am free within Your loving borders. Guide me on Your path of righteousness to a wide-open place. You are so good. You prepare a table for me there. You show me how to sit down and receive Your healing, provision, wisdom, longevity and all Your gifts of salvation."

Jesus' Words that Point to this Commandment

Matthew 11:16-24, Matthew 12:41-42, Matthew 23:37-38, Mark 6:11, Luke 3:9, Luke 10:12-16, Luke 11:31-32, John 5:22-24, John 12:48

And Jesus prayed this prayer:
"Father, thank you, for You are the Lord, the Supreme Ruler over heaven and earth! And You have hidden the great revelation of Your authority from those who are proud and wise in their own eyes. Instead You have shared it with those who humble themselves. Yes, Father, Your plan delights Your heart, as You have chosen this way to extend Your kingdom-by giving it to those who have become like trusting children." Matthew 11:25-26 TPT

How can I apply this to my life?

____

____

____

____

____

____

____

Are You Tired? Come Close to Me and Rest.

Red Letters

Jesus said, "Are you weary, carrying a heavy burden? Then come to Me.
I will refresh your life, for I am your oasis.
Simply join your life with Mine.
Learn My ways and you'll discover that I am gentle (peaceful) and humble...You will find...rest in Me." Matthew 11:28 TPT

Are you weighed down with condemnation and exhausted from beating yourself up? Come to Him and let His grace pick you up. You were never called to be perfect in your own strength. You were called to walk with Him. He is strength perfected.

Maybe you have separated yourself from the world, shared the gospel with opposition, walked through the storms of life, resisted sin, chose what was right (even though it was difficult) and you are tired physically and spiritually. Jesus commands you to come to Him and rest.

It is not a commandment for the weak, but for the strong.

Step away from living in the world and find rest for your soul by being in the care of your Savior. If your life is one battle after another, without pause, you are not obeying Jesus. Rest in His presence often.

Even if we are doing His work, He commands us to pause and release the cares and responsibilities that so easily latch on to us. He commands us to take His burden on us, which is easy and light. It is filled with love.

Take a deep breath and allow Him to lead you to a wide-open space, near still and restful waters. He will show you the grace gift of His righteousness. He will restore your soul. He will give you a new wind of supernatural strength.

Think of it as a regular pit stop as you travel on His paths of righteousness (Psalm 23).

Prayer

"Jesus, I receive Your gift of rest. I will be still and know You are God. Thank you that with each deep breath I take in Your beautiful Presence, my burdens are released. Holy Spirit, You are my Friend and Comforter."

Jesus' Words that Point to this Commandment

Matthew 11:28-30, Mark 6:30-31, John 16:33

> *Then Jesus suggested, "Let's get away from the crowds for a while and rest." Mark 6:31 TLB*

How can I apply this to my life?

____

____

____

____

____

____

____

____

Lord Yahweh, the Holy One of Israel, says: "Come back to Me! By returning and resting in Me you will be saved. In quietness and trust you will be made strong." Isaiah 30:15 TPT

Do Not Tempt Anyone to Sin.

Red Letters

And [Jesus] said to His disciples, "Temptations (snares, traps set to entice to sin) are sure to come, but woe to him by or through whom they come! It would be more profitable for him if a millstone were hung around his neck and he were hurled into the sea than that he should cause to sin or be a snare to one of these little ones lowly in rank or influence]." Luke 17:1-2 AMP

Things that tempt people to sin are an inevitable part of the world, but to that person who causes another to sin, Jesus says they will be met with great destruction.

Never lead anyone away from God.
Never be a part of anything that draws the weak into sin.

Jesus said to his friend Peter, when He sensed Peter was unconsciously tempting Him to defy His Father's will, "Get behind me Satan! You are a stumbling block to me; you do not have in mind the concerns of God, but merely human concerns" (Matthew 16:23). Peter was probably shocked at this statement, but his thoughtless words were dangerous. If Jesus accepted them, they would have weakened His faith and altered the will of God for His life.

Your example, your words, your investments, your choices are either pointing others to God or away.

Jesus says, "Woe to the person who does the tempting" (Matthew 18:7).

This means that an onslaught of sorrow, grief, calamities, troubles and afflictions will come on them.

Prayer

"Lord, I receive Your covering of righteousness. I repent of my sins and receive your forgiveness and freedom right now. I have the mind of Christ and my life is covered with Yours. Help me lead others to Your righteousness."

Jesus' Words that Point to this Commandment

Matthew 16:23, Matthew 18:6-7, Mark 9:42, Luke 17:1-2

> *But ask the Lord Jesus Christ to help you live as you should, and don't make plans to enjoy evil. Romans 13:14 TLB*

How can I apply this to my life?

____

____

____

____

____

____

____

____

____

And this is His command: to believe in the name of the Son, Jesus Christ, and to love one another as He commanded us. 1 John 3:23

Treat Children Well.

Red Letters

"Beware that you do not despise or feel scornful toward or think little of one of these little ones, for I tell you that in heaven their angels always are in the presence of and look upon the face of My Father Who is in heaven." Matthew 18:10 AMP

Jesus made a point of giving His undivided attention to little kids.
He chose to listen to them with love and He enjoyed them.
Of all the people on earth, they are the least powerful, but Jesus said, "Heaven belongs to them" (Matthew 18:3).

Children's natural instincts are honest, curious, and creative.
As believers, we could learn from them. We could learn to be more trusting, more teachable, and understand how to experience the freedom Jesus told us to walk in through their example.

In reality, adults are made from their experiences as children. Our words live in the foundation of a child's heart. Our criticisms and encouragement shape their personality and children often see the world through the eyes of their elders.

Just like the disciples, we sometimes find ourselves brushing children aside as unimportant. Instead, follow Jesus and take time to teach them and pray for them.

God pays special attention to how you treat them.

Prayer

"Lord, give me a heart for children. Open my eyes and ears to them.

Give me life-giving words to share a perfect 'word in season' to them. Help me take the time to lock eyes with them and see Your kingdom."

Jesus' Words that Point to this Commandment

Matthew 18:10, Matthew 19:13-14, Mark 9:36-37,42, Mark 10:13-16, Luke 17:1-2

> *Then He placed a little child among them; and taking the child in His arms he said to them, "Anyone who welcomes a little child like this in My name is welcoming Me, and anyone who welcomes Me is welcoming My Father who sent Me!" Mark 9:36-37 TLB*

How can I apply this to my life?

____

____

____

____

____

____

____

____

You unhappy one, storm-tossed and troubled, I am ready to rebuild you with precious stones and embed your foundations with sapphires. I will make your towers of rubies, your gates of sparkling jewels, and all your walls of precious delightful stones. All your children will be taught of Yahweh, and great will be their peace and prosperity. You will be established in righteousness. Oppression- be far from them! Fear-be far from them! Yes, terror will not come near you, nor will you be afraid. Isaiah 54:11-14 TPT

Get in the Game.

Red Letters

Jesus said, "Whoever is not with me is against me, and whoever does not gather with me scatters." Luke 11:23 NIV

There are two teams on the field.
You are on one team or the other. There are no bleachers. There are no cheerleaders. There are no onlookers hanging on the fence.

Calling yourself a Christian means you are in the huddle and Jesus is calling the plays. Your effort counts for the whole body of Christ. When you pray according to the Word, all of Heaven is behind you.

Don't be the distracted player that stands there looking to the other side and saying, "We're all just here to have fun and do what feels right." And wham! The enemy will tackle you, knock your socks off and take everything you love.

There is no closet Christianity. You either believe He is Lord of all or don't. You either believe what He said is absolute Truth or don't. Do not be counted among the people who will formulate a "Christianity" that suits their own passions according to 2 Timothy 4:3.

When you follow Christ, you follow ALL His teaching.

Being a Jesus follower means you make the decision to join your life with His. You are no longer your own.
You are not a true believer if you pick and choose how much of Jesus you agree with and want to represent.

To these, Jesus says, "On the day of judgement many will say to me, 'Lord, Lord, don't You remember us?' But I will have to say to them, 'Go away from Me, you lawless rebels! I've never been joined to you!'" (Matthew 7:22-23 TPT)

Prayer

"Lord, I am with You. When I chose You, I became a part of the victorious team. I am not the double-minded person who is tossed around with the changing ideologies of this world. Your Word is the playbook for my life."

Jesus' Words that Point to this Commandment

Matthew 4:18-20, Matthew 12:30, Luke 9:50, Luke 11:23, John 12:26

> *Jesus said, "Anyone who isn't helping me is harming me."*
> *Matthew 12:30 TLB*

How can I apply this to my life?

____

____

____

____

____

____

____

____

____

Do not merely listen to the Word, and so deceive yourselves. Do what it says. James 1:22

Be on Your Guard Against Division.

Red Letters

"Pay attention and always be on your guard [looking out for one another]. If your brother sins (misses the mark), solemnly tell him so and reprove him, and if he repents (feels sorry for having sinned), forgive him." Luke 17:3 AMP

Pay special attention to any issue that divides believers.
It is the enemy's number one weapon.
The Holy Spirit tells us in the book of James, "Where envying and strife (division) is, there is confusion and every evil work" (James 3:16). Where there is division in any situation, the enemy is at work.

Division in the body of Christ is a serious matter and Jesus makes it very clear how we should handle it.

He tells us if another Christian wrongs you, go to that person and tell them so. Don't hold it in. Hopefully they will apologize, and forgiveness, love and compassion will join two friends again.

If there is no apology, tell a few close Christians you trust about the matter so that you will have another perspective. (Sometimes our judgement is "off", and these witnesses will let us know.) If they agree, go together to the person, and address the issue again with humility.

If the person still does not apologize, bring the matter to church leadership you both trust and if that doesn't bring repentance-you may release the friendship.

The point of this whole process is to avoid small miscommunications that lead to offense and break up Christian friendships.

Our unity is Jesus' weapon.

<u>Prayer</u>

"Lord, when offense comes, I will submit to Your commandment. You have reconciled me to the Father, I will do my part to keep that reconciliation as a part of my lifestyle. I know that other believers are not my enemy. Open my eyes to the schemes of the wicked one to cause division."

<u>Jesus' Words that Point to this Commandment</u>

Matthew 6:14-15, Matthew 18:15-22, Matthew 20:24-28, Luke 17:3-4, John 20:23

> *Jesus said, "If your brother sins, go and show him his fault in private; if he listens and pays attention to you, you have won back your brother. But if he does not listen, take along with you one or two others, so that every word may be confirmed by the testimony of two or three witnesses. If he pays no attention to them [refusing to listen and obey], tell it to the church; and if he refuses to listen even to the church, let him be to you as a Gentile (unbeliever) and a tax collector." Matthew 18:15-17 AMP*

How can I apply this to my life?

___

___

___

___

___

___

___

Pray Together.

Red Letters

Jesus said, "What you say to one another is eternal. I mean this. When two of you get together on anything at all on earth and make a prayer of it, my Father in heaven goes into action. And when two or three of you are together because of Me, you can be sure that I'll be there."
Matthew 18:20 MSG

There is a time to pray in secret and there is a time to pray together. In the scripture above, Jesus is making it very clear that when you join your prayer with another believer and come before your heavenly Father in agreement, God's power will *always* come on the scene.

Our heavenly Father loves when we agree in prayer. Agreement gets His attention! He sent Jesus so that whosoever believes in Him would be part of the family of God: one body, one church, all in unity.

His pleasure is similar to a mother or father who are blessed when their children get into agreement for the good of the family.

In the beginning of the church, the new believers met to pray. They didn't plan services or raise money to build a building. Their first plan of action was to pray together even before they were baptized in the Holy Spirit.

We have the Holy Spirit now and when we pray with other believers, power from heaven flows through us. When we pray in agreement with each other and in agreement with the Word, we can be confident the One who created it all hears us.

When we pray together in the name of Jesus, our Messiah, He says,

"I promise to be there, and your request will be done."

There is so much power in agreement prayers! Seek out other believers and begin to change the world.

Prayer

"Lord, I commit today to find fellow believers and pray with them. Guide me to those who are like-minded in their love for You. I look forward to the amazing works You will accomplish when we pray in agreement."

Jesus' Words that Point to this Commandment

Matthew 18:19-20, John 14:13-20, John 15:16-17, John 16:23-28, John 17:26

> *Jesus prayed, "And I have revealed You (Father) to them (believers) and will keep on revealing You so that the mighty love you have for Me may be in them, and I in them." John 17:26 TLB*

How can I apply this to my life?

____

____

____

____

____

____

____

____

____

____

Be Like a Child.

Red Letters

The people brought children to Jesus, hoping he might touch them. The disciples shooed them off. But Jesus was irate and let them know it: "Don't push these children away. Don't ever get between them and me. These children are at the very center of life in the kingdom. Mark this: Unless you accept God's kingdom in the simplicity of a child, you'll never get in." Then, gathering the children up in his arms, he laid his hands of blessing on them. Mark 10:14-16 MSG

Trust.

It means to have a firm belief in the reliability, truth, ability, or strength of someone or something. The greatest trust is between a child and their loving parent or caregiver.

A child doesn't ask how you will care for them, they just know you will.
A child will freely express their joy in your presence.
A child will forgive quickly and move on.
A child doesn't focus on the cares of tomorrow, they live in the moment.
A child will hold you to your promise.
A child doesn't suggest the solution to a problem, they trust you have the answer.

To enter the very center of the Kingdom of God, you need to return to the trust of a little child. You need to remember what it was like to walk in the shadow of someone who is more powerful than you.

You need to listen to your loving Father, hear His word and confidently trust His promises. Your heart must release control and rest in God, your

Father. Take His hand. Crawl into His lap. Trust Him with all of your heart. His plan for you is good and His protection over you is perfect.

Jesus tells us to learn from a child and see with a pure heart.
When you do this, you will see God, and there is no darkness in Him.

Prayer

"Lord, I come to You as a little child. You are a perfect Father and I can trust You with all of my heart. You are the giver of every perfect gift. You would never harm me or take away something I loved. Your thoughts toward me are filled with love. Bless me today Abba Father (Papa)."

Jesus' Words that Point to this Commandment

Matthew 5:8, Matthew 5:44-45, Matthew 18:3, Matthew 19:14, Mark 10:14-16, Luke 18:16-17, Luke 20:35-36

> *Jesus said, "Happy are those whose hearts are pure, for they shall see God." Matthew 5:8 TLB*

How can I apply this to my life?

____

____

____

____

____

____

____

____

____

____

Do What God Tells You.

Red Letters

Another day, a man stopped Jesus and asked, "Teacher, what good thing must I do to get eternal life?" Jesus said, "Why do you question me about what's good? God is the One who is good.
If you want to enter the life of God, just do what He tells you."
Matthew 19:16-17 MSG

When you accepted Jesus as Lord of your life, your entire spirit changed. It became joined to Jesus and in that moment your spirit was resurrected with His and reborn by the Spirit of God. Your spiritual DNA changed, and you received, in addition to other gifts, spiritual ears. These spiritual ears allow you to hear the voice of God concerning your life.
He speaks to you in big and small things.

He is able to direct your path in life, but you have the choice to listen to Him and follow His direction.

His voice is not loud and most often does not drown out the noise of the world. You need to tune your ear to hear Him. You do this by prayer, meditating on the Word, and being quiet.

When He gives you direction, follow Him.
If He tell you to forgive someone, do it.
If He tells you to re-examine a problem in the light of His Word, do it.
If He tells you to share what He has done in your life to a stranger, follow through with it.

Very often, He waits for you to follow His direction and stays silent until you do.

Someone once prayed, "How do I hurt the devil?" and God answered, "It's the same way you bring Me sorrow, just don't do what he tells you to do."

Do what God tells you to do. When you do, you will be blessed.

<u>Prayer</u>

"Lord, I choose to be quiet and hear Your voice today. There is no wisdom above Yours."

<u>Jesus' Words that Point to this Commandment</u>

Matthew 19:16-17, Mark 4:24-25, Mark 10:17-22, Luke 18:18-30, John 5:25-30, John 8:47, John 10:14-16, John 10:27-30

> *Jesus said,*
> *'My sheep hear my voice, and I know them, and they follow me."*
> *John 10:27 KJV*

How can I apply this to my life?

____

____

____

____

____

____

____

____

Remove Your Accepted Limits.

Red Letters

Jesus said unto him,

"[You say to Me,] 'If You can?'

All things are possible for the one who believes and trusts [in Me]!"

Mark 9:23 AMP

What limits have you put on your future?
Are you too old? Too young? Too poor? Too tied down with responsibilities? Too dependent? Are you from the wrong side of town? Too tall? Too short? Too simple?

Jesus took the simple ones and changed the world.
He took the little boy's five loaves and two fish and fed five thousand.
He said to the paralyzed man who sat by the healing pool, "You don't need someone strong enough to help you, I am here."

Allow yourself to dream. See yourself doing what seems impossible. Release the accepted limits. Don't be afraid of disappointment. There is life in the vision.

Your next step is to believe and trust in Jesus. He will bring wisdom to the vision. When He says it is time to take the first step, He will be right there to help you stand.

When He walked the earth, He changed the natural with the supernatural and used the weak to bring down the strong. And He is still the same Jesus.

You do not need more money to make it possible. You do not need more influence to make it possible. You do not need more intelligence or talent.

You need to take your vision to your God, who is unlimited.
With God ALL things are possible. Listen. He will give you your first step.

<u>Prayer</u>

"Lord, forgive me for putting limits on what You can do with my life. I submit to You every fear, including the fear of failure. Here is my dream. Give me the first step. I know You will never leave me."

<u>Jesus' Words that Point to this Commandment</u>

Matthew. 9:28-29, Matthew 19:26, Mark 5:36, Mark 9:23, Mark 10:27, Luke 8:50, Luke 18:27, John 14:12-14

> *But Jesus beheld them, and said unto them, "With men this is impossible; but with God all things are possible." Matthew 19:26 KJV*

How can I apply this to my life?

Know That I See Your Sacrifices for My Sake and the Gospels, and You Will Have Your Reward.

Red Letters

And Jesus answered and said, "Verily I say unto you, there is no man that hath left house, or brethren, or sisters, or father, or mother, or wife, or children, or lands, for my sake, and the gospel's, but he shall receive an hundredfold now in this time, houses, and brethren, and sisters, and mothers, and children, and lands, with persecutions;
and in the world to come eternal life."
Mark 10:29-30

Following Jesus and obeying His commandments sometimes requires us to walk away from what the world would say are golden opportunities. Our heart sinks when we realize our walk with Him would be compromised if we do not walk away. The feeling of loss is real.
But He gives us this promise: God will not be out-given (Luke 6:38).

He says if we give up things to follow Him, we will be rewarded not only in Heaven but in this life as well. See your sacrifice as a seed to new gifts.

If you have had to walk away from family, career, business opportunities, dating relationships, prestigious positions, etc., to follow Jesus, His promise to you is this: you will receive a hundred times what you have given up.
Not double, but a hundred times. Not only in Heaven, but today.

Remember, your Heavenly Father isn't requiring you to give up what is eternally valuable. He is promising us real treasure when we walk through the narrow gate to follow Jesus.

Receive this promise and trust He has something better. A hundred times better.

Prayer

"Lord, You said to carry the cross and follow You. I put on the cross the things I hold tightly to because of fear. I put on the cross selfish desires that fuel me to get what I deserve. Your ways are so much better than mine. Break the chain of fear off of me and help me do what is right. I know Your blessing will chase me down."

Jesus' Words that Point to this Commandment

Matthew 5:10-12, Matthew 6:19-20, Matthew 16:24-27, Mark 8:35-38, Mark 10: 29-30, Luke 18:29-30, Luke 22:28-30

But calling the crowd to join his disciples, Jesus said, "Anyone who intends to come with me has to let me lead. You're not in the driver's seat; I am. Don't run from suffering; embrace it...What good would it do to get everything you want and lose you, the real you? What could you ever trade your soul for?"

Mark 8:35 MSG

How can I apply this to my life?

____

____

____

____

____

____

____

Don't Be Competitive with Other Christians.

Red Letters

When the other ten heard of this conversation, they lost their tempers with James and John. Jesus got them together to settle things down. "You've observed how godless rulers throw their weight around," he said, "and when people get a little power how quickly it goes to their heads. It's not going to be that way with you. Whoever wants to be great must become a servant. Whoever wants to be first among you must be your slave. That is what the Son of Man has done: He came to serve, not to be served—and then to give away his life in exchange for many who are held hostage." Mark 10:41-45 MSG

Walking in the "flesh" means you are empowered by your own abilities. The ways of the flesh begin with selfish ambition and lead to pride and corruption. You were not called to enjoy the fellowship of Jesus only to continue to walk in the flesh. We now walk in the unity of the Spirit.

What would you think if your right hand wanted to be greater than your left? Or if your left foot wanted to be faster than your right? There would be no coordination.

When you became a believer in Jesus, you were filled with the same Holy Spirit as your fellow believer. We are one body in Christ. We work together for good and serve one another in love.

The power to change the world rests in the Holy Spirit: "It is not by might nor by power, but by My Spirit says the Lord" (Zechariah 4:6).

Our work here on earth is to work together to bring the good news to all men and to equip the believers. There is no hierarchy in the Christian faith. We are one body called to servanthood.

Do not seek recognition and honor in the church. Seek to serve.

When God moves, He will move through men.
Never mistake the power of God as your power.

Prayer

"Lord, I lay aside any competitive nature I may have toward other believers. I know that jealousy is not from You. You have planted me where I am, to be a part of the body of Christ. I humbly come before You, offering my life as a sacrifice. My own works will not exalt me, but You will exalt me in due time."

Jesus' Words that Point to this Commandment

Matthew 5:16, Matthew 19:30, Matthew 20:1-16, Mark 10:35-45, John 15:12-13

> *Jesus said,*
> *"This is My commandment, that you love and unselfishly seek the best for one another, just as I have loved you. No one has greater love [nor stronger commitment] than to lay down his own life for his friends."*
> *John 15:12-13 AMP*

How can I apply this to my life?

____

____

____

____

____

____

____

____

Do Not Make Bargaining Prayers with God.

Red Letters

Jesus said, "Don't bargain with God. Be direct. Ask for what you need. This isn't a cat-and-mouse, hide-and-seek game we're in. If your child asks for bread, do you trick him with sawdust? If he asks for fish, do you scare him with a live snake on his plate? As bad as you are, you wouldn't think of such a thing. You're at least decent to your own children. So, don't you think the God who conceived you in love will be even better?"

Matthew 7:7-11 MSG

When you pray, be clear. Take off the cloak of fake holiness.
Do not bargain with Him. You have nothing new to offer Him.

When you gave Him your life in the prayer of salvation you held nothing back. When you gave Him your life, He received it.
He <u>will</u> care for you.

You have entered into the everlasting covenant He formed through the shed blood of Jesus Christ. You are as much a son or daughter to Him as Jesus. Come boldly, in prayer, to His throne of grace and lay down your desires before Him (Hebrews 4:16).

When you find promises in His Word concerning your situation and then boldly unite them with your petitions, God is pleased. He enjoys your faith.

He takes no pleasure in your begging and bargaining.

Remember what the Holy Spirit tells you in Romans 8:16, "For the Holy Spirit makes God's fatherhood real to you as He whispers into your innermost being, "You are God's beloved child!'" Instead of pleading with Him as an outsider, draw close to your Father and place your trust in Him. Wait in delightful expectation to see how He will bring those answers to pass. While you wait, daily thank Him for His faithfulness even before you see the victorious outcome.

Prayer

"Lord, I come boldly into Your throne room of unlimited grace. You purchased this robe of righteousness for me and I wear it. You call me Your child, a son and daughter of the Most High God and I receive it. Jesus, put me in right standing with You. There is nothing I can do to win more favor from You. Thank you, Jesus!"

Jesus' Words that Point to this Commandment

Matthew 6:7-13, Matthew 7:7-8, Matthew 21:21-22, Luke 11:1-13, John 14:13-14, John 15:7-8, John 15:16

> *Jesus said,*
> *"You have not chosen Me, but I have chosen you and I have appointed and placed and purposefully planted you, so that you would go and bear fruit and keep on bearing, and that your fruit will remain and be lasting, so that whatever you ask of the Father in My name [as My representative] He may give to you." John 15:16 AMP*

How can I apply this to my life?

____

____

____

____

____

____

Don't Ask for More Faith.

Red Letters

But the Master said, "You don't need more faith. There is no 'more' or 'less' in faith. If you have a bare kernel of faith, say the size of a poppy seed, you could say to this sycamore tree, 'Go jump in the lake,' and it would do it." Luke 17:6 MSG

What mountain stands in front of you that seems higher than your ability to pray and see it disappear? What deadly tree, standing before you, has dug its roots so deep into the earth that it seems immovable?

When you made the decision to believe in God, you connected to the One who made it all. That connection is faith.
Don't ask for more faith just as you wouldn't ask for another connection.

That connection to God CAN be strengthened by every promise He has made in His Word. Hearing and reading God's word keeps that connection strong and purifies it from the destructive threads of doubt. That strong connection will give you a voice to call the things "that be not, as though they were" (Romans 4:17).

Just as a polluted pond will not be purified with more water, your faith can only be purified by removing doubt.

Questions that you allow to cross your mind regarding God's ability to answer your prayer feed doubt and doubt eats away at faith. Be aware, when doubt enters your thoughts, the only thing that can fend it off is God's Word.

This is the battle you must fight.
Faith without doubt is the most powerful force on earth.

Prayer

"Lord, I believe. I believe You are the One who spoke, and the worlds were formed. I believe there is no one higher than You. I believe Your understanding is above my understanding. I believe the plans You have for me are good; to deliver me, heal me, and prosper me. Forgive me for doubting You."

Jesus' Words that Point to this Commandment

Matthew 17:20-21, Matthew 21:21-22, Mark 4:30-32, Mark 11:22-24, Luke 13:18-21, Luke 17:6

> *"Why could we not drive it out?" Jesus answered, "Because of your little faith [your lack of trust and confidence in the power of God]; for I assure you and most solemnly say to you, if you have [living] faith the size of a mustard seed, you will say to this mountain, 'Move from here to there,' and [if it is God's will] it will move; and nothing will be impossible for you."*
>
> *Matthew 17:20 AMP*

How can I apply this to my life?

____

____

____

____

____

____

____

Find Your Identity in God's Word.

Red Letters

Follow Me in this:

"Don't suppose for a minute that I have come to demolish the Scriptures—either God's Law or the Prophets. I'm not here to demolish but to complete. I am going to put it all together, pull it all together in a vast panorama. God's Law is more real and lasting than the stars in the sky and the ground at your feet. Long after stars burn out and earth wears out, God's Law will be alive and working."

Matthew 5:18 MSG

Jesus studied the Word of God. This is a marvelous mystery because He was "the Word that became flesh and dwelt among us "(John 1:14).

He established every truth from the beginning yet, in the body, Jesus searched the scriptures and found the truth about who He was. He also knew what the scriptures said about His enemy. He responded to the enemy with, "It is written..." He knew the power of God's written Word in the earthly realm.

He knew His Father intimately through the sacred teachings and spending dedicated time in prayer. He knew what to expect in the future because of the Word.

He knew God's will for His life. He walked in every promise.

Jesus knew that the Word of God is alive because it is written by the Living breath of God. He knew it was powerful in Its truth, like a weapon.

We are called to follow Him in this.

Read it, study it, meditate on it. Receive it and it will uphold your life.
Find out who you are in the Word of God.
Your life should reflect His Word.

Do you believe you are more than a conqueror through Christ who loves you? You are. Do you believe there is no condemnation over your life if you are in Christ Jesus? There isn't.
Find these truths and find your identity.

Prayer

"Lord, I am who You say I am. Wash away all the labels people have spoken over my life. Help me walk in this new perspective. My life is hidden in Your Word."

Jesus' Words that Point to this Commandment

Matthew 4:4,7,10,13-17, Matthew 5:17-18, Matthew 5:33,38, Matthew 11:3-6,10, Matthew 13:14-15, Matthew 21:1-5,13, Matthew 24:34-35, Matthew 26:24, Matthew 26:31-32,56, Mark 7:6, Mark 9:12-13, Luke 4:8-30,43, John 6:45

> *But Jesus told him, "No! For the Scriptures tell us that bread won't feed men's souls: obedience to every word of God is what we need."*
> *Matthew 4:4 TLB*

How can I apply this to my life?

____

____

____

____

____

____

Sit in a Humble Place.

Red Letters

Jesus said,
"All those who exalt themselves will be humbled, and those who humble themselves will be exalted." Luke 18:14 NIV

Pride will always produce foolishness.
Although you are a child of the Almighty God, sit in a humble place.
Even in your humility, you will be acknowledged as royalty. You are called a son and daughter of the Almighty God.

The wise know it is best to listen and observe rather than speak. Jesus is reminding us of Proverbs 15:33, "Humility precedes honor."

The focus of a person who is without God, is always on self-promotion. Their god is self. They are lost to nothingness if they do not succeed and make a name for themselves. Your focus is on promotion of Almighty God. As you lift Him up, He lifts you up.

Your humility is accepting you are the Lord's and He is your Savior.

This humility is not focused on putting yourself down. Instead it is focusing on those things you think you can do <u>without</u> God and then surrendering them to Him. The Holy Spirit says in James 4:10 (TPT), "Be willing to be made low before the Lord and He will exalt you!"

True humility acts in obedience to His Word.
True humility allows Him to execute justice.

True humility draws you closer to the throne of the Father who crowns you with authority and everlasting life.

Prayer

"Lord, I am Yours. I will serve as You serve. I will love as You love. My desire is to see You glorified in my life. I surrender everything I have held tightly with pride. Help me walk humbly with You."

Jesus' Words that Point to this Commandment

Matthew 20:27-28, Matthew 21:5-11, Matthew 23:12, Matthew 24:46, Mark 9:35, Mark 10:31, Mark 10:43-45, Luke 1:52, Luke 12:35-38, Luke 13:29-30, Luke 14:11, Luke 18:14, Luke 22:27-30, John 7:18, John 8:54

> *And He sat down and called the Twelve [apostles], and He said to them, "If anyone desires to be first, he must be last of all, and servant of all."*
> *Mark 9:35 AMP*

How can I apply this to my life?

____

____

____

____

____

____

You are always and dearly loved by God! So robe yourself with virtues of God, since you have been divinely chosen to be holy. Be merciful as you endeavor to understand others, and be compassionate, showing kindness toward all. Be gentle and humble...Colossians 3:12 TPT

Be Moved by the Things That Make God Angry.

Red Letters

Follow Me in this:

And Jesus went into the temple of God and cast out all them that sold and bought in the temple, and overthrew the tables of the moneychangers, and the seats of them that sold doves, and said unto them, "It is written, My house shall be called the house of prayer; but ye have made it a den of thieves." And the blind and the lame came to him in the temple; and he healed them.

Matthew 21:12-14 KJV

God is angry when religious ideas burden people.
He is also angry when man creates laws that go against His will.
God is angry when men, who claim to be godly, hurt people.

Some other things that make God angry are "prideful, self-intoxicated people, a liar, one who murders the innocent, people who spend their time making evil plans, people who run toward anything evil, people who omit the truth to deceive others, and people who cause division" (Proverbs 6:16-19).

When was the last time you were angry? If you are anything like me, it might have had more to do with pride than what makes God angry.

Jesus anger was always righteous, and it never lasted.
In the scripture above, He reacts to the injustice with a declaration of what is true. His anger led Him to declare the Word of God.
Human emotions need the rock of the Word to stabilize the heart.
Immediately after, Jesus moved in with love.

He was instantly ready to focus on healing those who were burdened. Righteous anger keeps its focus on healing, not on destruction. Follow Him in this.

Prayer

"Lord, I give you my heart. Cleanse me from unrighteous passions. Stir up in me a passion to change those things that are close to Your heart."

Jesus' Words that Point to this Commandment

Matthew 14:14, Matthew 21:12-14, Mark 3:4-6. Mark 11:15-17, Luke 13:10-17, Luke 14:1-4

> *He asked them, "Is it lawful on the Sabbath to do good or to do evil, to save a life or to kill?" But they kept silent. After looking around at them with anger, grieved at the hardness and arrogance of their hearts, He told the man, "Hold out your hand." And he held it out, and his hand was [completely] restored. Mark 3:4-5 AMP*

How can I apply this to my life?

Offer a Sacrifice of Praise to God.

Red Letters

From the Throne (of the King of kings) came a shout, a command:
"Praise our God, all you his servants, all you who fear him,
small and great!"
Then I heard the sound of massed choirs, the sound of a mighty cataract, the sound of strong thunder: "Hallelujah! The Master reigns, our God, the Sovereign-Strong! Let us celebrate, let us rejoice, let us give him the glory!" Revelation 19:5-8 MSG

You have been commanded to worship God which means to let go of yourself and completely adore Him. Worship involves your humility and your ability to surrender.
Praise is different.

Your offering of praise comes from a thankful heart. It is the action of the one leper (out of the ten who were healed) who returned to Jesus to say, "Thank you!" We thank Him for all he has done, what He is doing, and what He is going to do.

NOW is the time to praise your Creator...with your whole being.
Even when you don't feel like it, make it your sacrifice to Him (Hebrews 13:15). Make a joyful noise to the Lord who has delivered you from darkness into His glorious light.

Don't let religious ideas complicate it. Jesus told us even a tiny baby can do it. We might even need to learn from them.

Pay attention to the joy of a baby responding to a loved one.

Respond to God this way.
There are no pretenses and no rules. Praise Him without self-consciousness. Lift your hands and praise Him with unquestionable trust and a whole-body response to His unconditional Love.

Prayer

"Praise Your wonderful Name! I adore You with all of my heart, Lord. Thank you for all You have done for me. Bless the Lord! You are so good! You have forgiven all my sins! You have healed all of my diseases! You have redeemed my life from the pit and You have crowned me with loving-kindness and tender mercy!"

Jesus' Words that Point to this Commandment

Matthew 21:9-11,16-17, Luke 10:21-27, Luke 17:11-19, Luke 19:35-40, John 12:12-18

> *Do You hear what these children are saying? they asked Him. "Yes," replied Jesus, "Have you never read, 'From the lips of children and infants, You Lord, have called forth Your praise?'"*
> *Matthew 21:16 NIV*

How can I apply this to my life?

____

____

____

____

____

____

____

____

Produce Eternal Fruit with Your Life.

Red Letters

And seeing from afar a fig tree having leaves (if there are leaves there should be fruit), He went to see if perhaps He would find something on it. When He came to it, He found nothing but leaves...
And Jesus answered and said unto it, "Let no one eat fruit from you ever again." And his disciples heard it. Mark 11:13-14 NKJV

Do not be a fruitless tree in the Kingdom of God who appears holy, but in reality, seeks only to have its needs met and lives only for itself.

God is love. His mercy and loving-kindness chase after you. He puts a ring on your finger, clothes you with Christ, and calls you His own (Luke 15:21-24). But the season will come when it is time for you to share with others what God has done in your life and make real changes in the world around you.

Jesus said, "Go preach what you hear from the Lord and stand up on top of your dwelling place and share it for all to hear!" (Matthew 10:27)

No one can argue with what has happened in your heart. No one can discount your experience. The most powerful witness of God's love is sharing your experience of receiving it.

In Isaiah 61:1-3 we read of a God-given anointing: "The Spirit of the Lord has anointed me to proclaim good news to the poor, to bind up the brokenhearted, to proclaim freedom to the captives...to bestow a crown of beauty for ashes, the oil of joy for mourning, and a garment of praise

for a spirit of despair. They (those who receive this anointing) will be called oaks of righteousness, planted by the Lord for His glory."
In Luke 4:16, Jesus reads this scripture and then sits down and says, "Today this scripture has been fulfilled in your hearing." Jesus has given you personal access to this anointing...today.

Bear good fruit with your life. Leave in your wake the God-kind of fruit: love, joy, peace, patience, kindness, goodness and self-control (Galatians 5:22). Decide to go outward with your faith and bless the Lord who has blessed you.

Prayer

"Lord, I lay at Your throne any fear of what man can say or do. Everywhere I go today I am prepared to share Your goodness. Let my life proclaim Psalm 34, 'Taste and see, the Lord is good!'"

Jesus' Words that Point to this Commandment

Matthew 10:27, Matthew 21:18-19, Matthew 12:33, Matthew 7:15- 21, Mark 5:19, Mark 11:13-14, John 15:4-11

> *"My true disciples produce bountiful harvests. This brings great glory to my Father." John 15:8 TLB*

How can I apply this to my life?

Be Clothed with Christ.

Red Letters

Jesus taught them, "There once was a king who arranged an extravagant wedding feast for his son. On the day the wedding festivities were set to begin, he sent his servants to summon all the invited guests, but they chose not to come. Then the king said, "...Now I want you to go into the streets and alleyways and invite anyone and everyone you find to come and enjoy the wedding feast in honor of my son. So, the servants went out and invited everyone to come to the wedding feast, good and bad alike, until the banquet hall was crammed with people! Now when the king entered the banquet hall...he noticed a guest who was not wearing the wedding robe provided for him. The king turned to his servants and said, 'Tie him up and throw him into the outer darkness where there will be great sorrow, with weeping and grinding of teeth.'"
Matthew 22:2-3, 10, 11-13 TPT

When Adam and Eve sinned and separated themselves from God, they knew they were naked. The precious garment of God, His glory, had left them. They looked for something to possess to protect and cover themselves. They gathered leaves and created their own, man-made garment. (Genesis 3:7)

When Moses came to the burning bush and God spoke to Him through it, He said, "Take off your sandals for the place you are standing is holy ground" (Exodus 3:5). God wanted Moses to remove what separated him from God's holy presence, his man-made sandals.

Jesus tells us, "If God so clothes the grass of the field...will He not much more clothe you?" (Matthew 6:30) God has provided a new garment for you to wear.

Jesus has clothed you with His salvation (Isaiah 61:10). He has taken off your filthy robe of sin and the tattered garment you have made for yourself. He has purchased for you, through the cross, a robe of righteousness. When you accepted Jesus as your Savior, He dressed you in a pure garment woven with His blood. You put on His forgiveness, His righteousness, His love, His faith and His joy. This is not to be taken lightly.

You wear the victorious garment of the Holy Spirit and only those who are dressed this way are given entrance to the wedding feast of the Lamb. What are you wearing that separates you from Him? Do not allow depression, fear, and worry to be your garment. Be clothed with Christ's victorious armor of light.

Prayer

"Lord, You have clothed Me with Your very best. Forgive me for putting on anything I have made for my own protection. You are my God. I wear Your holiness and not my own."

Jesus' Words that Point to this Commandment

Matthew 6:25-34, Matthew 11:28-30, Matthew 22:2-14, Luke 12:24-34, Luke 24:49, John 3:16

> *Jesus said, "I am going to send you what my Father has promised; but stay in the city until you have been clothed with power from on high."*
> *Luke 24:49 NIV*

How can I apply this to my life?

____

____

____

____

____

Respect Authority.

Red Letters

Jesus answering said unto them, "Render to Caesar the things that are Caesar's, and to God the things that are God's."
And they marveled at him. Mark 12:17 KJV

When the Pharisees came to Jesus with the question, "Is it lawful to give tribute (honor with your money) to Caesar?" They meant to trap Him. He knew this, so He asked them whose image was on the coin. They said, "Caesar", so He said, "Then give to Caesar what is his," but then added a commandment, "And give to God the things that are God's."

We live in a world where governments are set in place to keep order. At the time, Caesar was head of the government. Jesus knows that we must live in the world, and at the same time be separated from it. He makes the distinction that we are not to be anarchists.
Pay your taxes, obey the laws that have been set in place to keep order, respect those who administer safety and pray for them daily.
Governments create monetary systems so our economy can function and Jesus, very practically, commands us to abide by those laws.

But the real heart of Jesus is what He said next: "Give everything that belongs to God back to God." The truth is, everything belongs to God because God made everything (John 1:3). When this life is over what will you pack up and take with you?

You are given the gift of life, made in His image, so reflect Him.
Give Him your life.

He is the Author and Finisher of your faith, so respect His *author*-ity.

Prayer

"Lord, I give you my life. Everything in this world that makes me anxious, I give to You. I lift up to You the rulers of this land, guide them so we, Your people, can live in peace. Guide me in Your truth and holiness as I walk this earth."

Jesus' Words that Point to this Commandment

Matthew 22:21, Matthew 25:14-30, Mark 12:17, Luke 20:25, John 12:25-26, John 17:13-26

> *Jesus prayed, "I have given them Your message and that is why the unbelieving world hates them. For their alliance is no longer to this world. I am not asking that You remove them from the world, but I ask that You guard their hearts from evil, for they no longer belong to the world any more than I do. Your Word is truth! So make them holy by Your truth. I have commissioned them to represent Me just as You commissioned Me to represent You." John 17:14-19 TLB*

How can I apply this to my life?

Red Letters

Jesus said unto her, "I am the resurrection, and the life: he that believeth in me, though he were dead, yet shall he live." John 11:25

God is not the God of the dead, but of the Living!
In Christ, you are alive. In Christ is abundant, resurrected life. If you are in Christ, you *can* reflect an abundant life.

Your spirit can be so soaked in His Word that you have wisdom for every circumstance. Jesus tells us in John 6:63 that the Word of God IS LIFE! Your soul can be so anchored in His promises that whenever emotions begin to flare up, you run to the shelter of those promises, no matter what comes your way.
Your body is not wired for weakness and sickness when you have Jesus in you. He is renewing youthful energy in you right now!

Remember these promises: You are made alive forever. Death has no hold on you. You will not even feel the sting of death (1 Corinthians 15:55-57). He has provided your every (earthly and spiritual) need through His riches and glory in Christ Jesus. You have supernatural abundance available to you for every area of life (Philippians 4:19). You can relax, your work is to just believe (John 6:29).

It is time to be spiritually led and not emotionally tossed around in life. Ask yourself, "What does the Word say about me?" Believe what Jesus said in His Word over what you feel.

Your born-again spirit is already an overcomer in this world. Jesus reminds you over and over to walk in that overcoming spirit because that

is where you will find your victory and truly live!
He is an extravagant God and gives you life extravagantly!

Prayer

"Today, Father, I breathe in Your beautiful life for me. Fill me with Your presence. My mind is a wide-open space filled with possibilities. My ears are open to the voice of Your Holy Spirit. I receive all that You have for me."

Jesus' Words that Point to this Commandment

Matthew 6: 31-33, Mark 9:23, Mark 12:24-27, Luke 20:38, John 3:16, John 5:24-25, John 6:47-51, John 10:10, John 11:25-26

> *"The thief (of life) comes only in order to steal and kill and destroy. I came that they may have and enjoy life, and have it in abundance [to the full, till it overflows]." John 10:10 AMP*

How can I apply this to my life?

Wherever I go I will thank you. All the nations will hear my praise songs to you. Your love is so extravagant, it reaches higher than the heavens! Your faithfulness is so astonishing, it stretches to the skies! Psalm 108:3-4

Seek Relationship Not Religion.

Red Letters

Jesus said, "These people draw near Me with their mouths and honor Me with their lips, but their hearts hold off and are far away from Me."
Matthew 15:8 AMP

Who you are is not defined by a certificate or a church.
Who you are is written on your heart.

You might be able to fool men, but God clearly sees what is written there. In 1 Samuel 16:7, the Holy Spirit tells us, "The Lord sees not as man sees; man looks on the outward appearance, but the Lord looks on the heart."

You might be able to quote the scriptures for every situation by memory and attend every holy day and sit in holy places, but if the Word is not deeply rooted and grounded in love within your inner man, you are simply a hypocrite.

Humble yourself in prayer and ask Him to show you who He is.
Seek His face, not religion. Get real with Him. Ask questions. Hear His voice and trust Him. He is a good Father.

Carving out real time in your day to develop relationship with Him will restore your soul and leave no room for buried resentment, anger, or fear. Time with Him will teach you what love really is: "How intimate is His love! How enduring and inclusive it is-this love is poured into you until you are filled to overflowing with the fullness of God" (Ephesians 3:18 TPT).

You will learn to speak with the "tongues of men and angels", and you will learn how to let your words be soaked with love (1 Corinthians 13).

Religion is man reaching to God...but a relationship with Jesus Christ is God reaching down to you.

Prayer

"Lord, I need You. When the day begins, I need Your wisdom and direction. Help me not hold the weight of my life. I am not strong enough. When the day ends, I will praise You for Your wonderful works. You are everything I need."

Jesus' Words that Point to this Commandment

Matthew 15: 1-20, Matthew 22:37-40, Mark 7:6-23, Mark 8:15-21, Mark 12:38-40, John 5:37-40

> *Jesus said, "You search the Scriptures, for you believe they give you eternal life. And the Scriptures point to me! Yet you won't come to me so that I can give you this life eternal!"*
>
> *John 5:39-40 TLB*

How can I apply this to my life?

Do Not be Fooled. When I Return, the Whole Earth will Know.

Red Letters

Jesus said,
"If they say to you, 'Look! He is in the wilderness,' do not go out there, or 'Look! He is in the inner rooms,' do not believe it. For just as the lightening comes from the east and flashes as far as the west, so will be the coming [in glory] of the Son of Man [everyone will see Him clearly]."
Matthew 24:26-27 AMP

When Jesus first came to earth as the Lamb of God, scripture says He "emptied Himself, taking the form of a bond-servant, and being made in the likeness of men" (Philippians 2:7).

He was tempted in the same things as you and I, but without sin. He walked the earth in gentle humility filled with grace and truth. He laughed and cried with us.

He became the required sacrifice and laid His sinless life down as a payment for the sins of the world. In perfect love He washed us clean. He took a crown of thorns that belonged to us. He willingly allowed Himself to be hung on a cross judged by men and God for disobedience that was not His. He was buried under the full weight of our judgement.

But the Spirit pierced through eternal darkness and filled Him with life again. He rose from death's locked grave, defeating all the powers of sin and death. And He took their authority over the world.

We became His Believers, a new creation. He gave us His crown of righteousness and called us to join Him in victory over death.
He now sits at the right hand of the Father of all Creation making our enemies His footstool. He intercedes for us and has given us His Holy

Spirit to guide us in all things.

But a day is coming, and it is called "The Day of the Lord". On that day the Lord Jesus will return to the earth, a mighty Warrior-Messiah, and ALL will know that He is King of kings and Lord of lords. All the earth and its inhabitants will know that *all* authority is His. He will come, not in one small corner of the world, but in plain sight for every man and woman on the earth to see: a planetary event.

Before this day comes, He warns us to beware of imitators who say, "I am the Christ." We are to watch for false teachers who spread rumors He has returned. We should be aware of powerful personalities that proclaim the ideal form of humanity, which is the antichrist movement.
Look up! Get ready! Know Christ. He will come in power for His victorious church and you WON'T miss Him.

Prayer

"Lord, I believe Your Word. I believe that every knee will bow and every tongue will confess You are Lord of all. I am looking forward to that day. But if today is not that day, I proclaim in all I do and think, You are Lord over my life.

Jesus' Words that Point to this Commandment

Matthew 24:4-28,36-39, Matthew 25:13, Matthew 24:44, Mark 13:5-6, 21,22, Luke 17:22-24, Luke 21:8-15, 25-28

> *Jesus said, "So when all these things begin to happen, stand straight and look up! For your salvation is near." Luke 21:28 TLB*

How can I apply this to my life?

____

____

Take Communion Regularly.

Red Letters

Taking bread, he blessed it, broke it, and gave it to them, saying, "This is my body, given for you. Eat it in my memory." He did the same with the cup after supper, saying, "This cup is the new covenant written in my blood, blood poured out for you."

Luke 22:19-20 MSG

When we take communion, we remember. We remember what Jesus has done for us on the cross. We remember our need for a Savior.

When we eat the bread, we remember He sacrificed His body so we can live forever. When we take the cup, we remember He poured out His blood to dissolve our sin and its power to destroy us. We remember our sins and repent. We remember that He promised us He will come again in glory.

The power of this action finds its roots in covenant relationship. When two covenant partners agreed to stand with each other and provide and protect one another, they sealed their agreement with a ceremonial meal. Jesus commands us to remember the covenant He secured for us by taking the bread and cup, regularly.

It doesn't need to be a specially prepared "wafer". It can be any edible representation of His body. What is important is the preparation of your heart. Begin by coming to the Father in the name of Jesus. Examine your heart (1 Corinthians 11:28).

Judge yourself according to God's Word and repent of areas you have sinned (missed the mark). Receive forgiveness because "He is faithful and just to forgive you" (1 John 1:9). And then release your forgiveness to those who have hurt you.

Read 2 Corinthians 5:21: "God made Him (Jesus) who had no sin to be sin for me, so that in Him I might become the righteousness of God." Read Matthew 26:26-28 and receive communion as the righteousness of God in Christ Jesus.

Finally, acknowledge the covenant that was ratified by the shed blood of Jesus at Calvary. His covenant agreement provides health for your body, forgiveness for sin, joy, protection, abundance, faith, peace, provision, wisdom, understanding, and everlasting life. Now receive the promise.

Prayer

"Lord, forgive me. I receive Your cleansing and now I take the bread because You are the Bread of Life. I receive all You have for me now and for eternity. I drink the cup and remember Your sacrifice. I am a partaker of the new covenant through the blood You shed on Calvary. Thank you."

Jesus' Words that Point to this Commandment

Matthew 26:26-29, Luke 22:19-20 Mark 14:22-25, John 6:33,35,48,51-58, Luke 24:30

> *Jesus said, "I am the living bread which came down from heaven: if any man eat of this bread, he shall live forever: and the bread that I will give is my flesh, which I will give for the life of the world." John 6:51 KJV*

How can I apply this to my life?

____

____

____

____

____

Reach Boldly with Your Faith and Grasp Your Miracle.

Red Letters

Now in the crowd that day was a woman who had suffered horribly from continual bleeding for twelve years. She had endured a great deal under the care of various doctors, yet in spite of spending all that she had on their treatments, she was not getting better but worse. When she heard about Jesus' healing power, she pushed through the crowd and came up from behind Him and touched His prayer shawl. For she kept saying to herself, "If only I could touch His clothes, I know I will be healed." As soon as her hand touched Him, her bleeding immediately stopped! She knew it, for she could feel her body instantly being healed of her disease!

Jesus knew at once that someone had touched Him, for He felt the power that always surged around Him had passed through for someone to be healed. He turned and spoke to the crowd, saying, "Who touched my clothes?" [Then] she came before Him, trembling with fear, and threw herself down at His feet saying, "I was the one who touched you."

Jesus said to her, "Daughter, because you dared to believe, your faith has healed you. Go with peace in your heart, and be free from your suffering!" Mark 5:25-30,33-34 TPT

Faith operates in confidence.

The woman who reached out to Jesus had total confidence that if she touched the prayer shawl Jesus wore, she would be healed. That prayer shawl had special borders and tassels that symbolized the promises and commandments of God. It also symbolized the healing wings of God. She had heard the report of the Messiah. She knew the Messiah would bring healing. She accepted the Word that He was her Healer.

She did not beg in prayer on the outskirts of a hungry crowd for Jesus to heal her. She did not wail and bring attention to her need, so He would focus on her and heal her. She accepted the fact He was her Healer and pursued Him.

She did not wait for Him to point to the crowd and say, "It is My will to heal.... you!" She reached out with confidence in who He was, and if He did it for someone else, He could do it for her.

What was His response? Joy. He was pleased she reached out by faith and was healed. Know your Savior. Know His promises. Dare to believe, reach boldly without fear and grasp your miracle. He says, "Yes and Amen! Live well! Live blessed!"

Prayer

"Lord, I believe You are my healer. I believe You can and will heal me. Today I reach out by faith and connect to Your anointing."

Jesus' Words that Point to this Commandment

Matthew 14:27-31, Mark 5:25-43, Mark 10:46-52, Luke 8:43-48, Luke 17:19, John 1:12

> *But to as many as did receive and welcome Him, He gave the right [the authority, the privilege] to become children of God, that is, to those who believe in (adhere to, trust in, and rely on) His name. John 1:12 AMP*

How can I apply this to my life?

____

____

____

____

____

____

Share Your Company with Those Who Need God.

Red Letters

Follow Me in this:

Jesus said, "I came not to call the righteous, but sinners to repentance."

Luke 5:32 KJV

Do others know you by your mercy? Mercy is kindness toward those who should be judged.

Pray for a heart that is merciful. A heart that sees the wounded soul in the undesirable. A heart that sees the wounded soul in arrogance. A heart that sees the wounded soul who can't escape their sin.

Jesus says to learn what this means: "I will have mercy, and not sacrifice" (Matthew 9:13). Read that again. Mercy triumphs over judgement of others (James 2:13). Mercy triumphs over religious attitudes.

Mercy embraces. Mercy is a beautiful response to something ugly. It is not an ugly response to what is ugly. Mercy speaks only what is nourishing and true over the weak. Mercy offers space without restrictions or time limits. Anger gets extinguished by mercy. Mercy seeks healing, not punishment, and does not wound the wounded. The voice of mercy doesn't call out to the godly, but to sinners...

Jesus displayed mercy perfectly.
Mercy is perfect leadership in the Kingdom of God.

God described Himself to Moses this way: "The Lord, the Lord God, merciful and gracious, longsuffering and abundant in goodness and truth, keeping mercy for thousands" (Exodus 34:5-6).

When we experience God's mercy, we can be merciful. Trying to be merciful without Jesus fueling that mercy is exhausting. You must be filled.

Never forget, it was His mercy that transformed you.
Following Jesus means you will go out of your circle of friends and spend time with those who need Jesus.

<u>Prayer</u>

"Lord, help me to 'remember my days are numbered and help me to interpret my life correctly' (Psalm 90:12). You have been so merciful to me. Give me Your eyes, Your ears, and Your heart for this lost and hurting world. Heal me from a constant state of self-centered busy-ness and give me eyes to see the person who might be caught in a ditch, waiting for their 'Good Samaritan' (Luke 10:25-37)."

<u>Jesus' Words that Point to this Commandment</u>

Matthew 6:14-15, Matthew 9:12-13, Luke 5:30-32, Luke 15:4-10, Luke 15:18-24, John 3:16

> *But none of these things move me, neither count I my life dear unto myself, so that I might finish my course with joy, and the ministry, which I have received of the Lord Jesus, to testify the gospel of the grace of God.*
> *Acts 20:24 KJV*

How can I apply this to my life?

____

____

____

____

____

____

Give Extravagantly to God.

Red Letters

"Just then Jesus looked up and saw the rich people dropping offerings in the collection plate. Then he saw a poor widow put in two pennies. He said, "The plain truth is that this widow has given by far the largest offering today. All these others made offerings that they'll never miss; she gave extravagantly what she couldn't afford—she gave her all!"
Luke 21:1-4 MSG

Before you can give extravagantly to God you need to give Him your heart. And when you do this, you place ALL your trust in Him. You trust Him beyond any amount of money this world could provide. You enter the faith-reality that He alone will sustain you and open the door of Heaven to bless you.

It isn't the amount on the check or the hours logged in that He notices. He notices the attitude of your heart. God measures wealth only by the heart.

The rich young millionaire ruler who was unwilling to give up his earthly riches to follow Jesus was a very poor soul in the eyes of our Lord (Mark 10:21-27). In God's eyes wealth is pure faith. It gets His attention.

Faith gives you access to the wealth of heaven which gives you access to abundance in every area of your life. The treasures of Heaven are eternal.

Give joyfully with an expectant, faith-filled heart. He doesn't need your money, he needs your heart, and if it trusts in riches, it doesn't trust in Him.

Prayer

"Lord, I give You my heart. I place no other gods before You. You sustain me. My giving is an opportunity for You to open the window of Heaven and pour a blessing on me I can't even contain."

Jesus' Words that Point to this Commandment

Matthew 6:1-4, 21, 24, Matthew 13:22,44-46, Matthew 19:21-29, Mark 12:43-44, Luke 6:38, Luke 11:39-44, Luke 12:33-34, Luke 16:10-15, Luke 21:3-4

Jesus said, "For where your treasure is, there will your heart be also." Matthew 6:21 KJV

How can I apply this to my life?

____

____

____

____

____

____

____

____

____

My delightfully loved friends, when our hearts don't condemn us, we have a bold freedom to speak face-to-face with God. And whatever we ask of Him we receive, because we keep His commands. And by our beautiful intentions we continue to do what brings pleasure to Him.

1 John 3:21 TPT

Do Not Trust in the World's System of Wealth.

Red Letters

Jesus said, "Children, it is next to impossible for those who trust in their riches to find their way into God's kingdom realm."
Mark 10:24 TPT

Worldly wealth finds safety behind gates and walls. It finds confidence in jewelry, clothing, and cars. Worldly wealth puts out a barrier from poverty. It places the person behind a false fortress of power.

Worldly wealth deceives. Trusting in the wealth of this world produces a spiritual callus. When sickness and death slide past those walls and take control, there is nowhere to turn.

Jesus warns us to not place our trust in worldly riches because they are not enough. Money is a false security. It is like a wall made with shifting sand.

True wealth is found in walking with Him. There is no greater security than eternal life with Him.

Every need is met when you walk with Christ: joy for sadness, freedom for oppression, peace for chaos, healing for pain, life for death.
"The blessing of the Lord makes a person rich, and He adds no sorrow with it" (Proverbs 10:22). Earthly goods will be added to you, but with joy... because you won't be ruled by them.

You will be blessed with finances, but your heart will not be kept by them.

Prayer

"Lord, my trust is in You. Thank you for wealth and riches in my household but I will not lean on them for security. They are tools to bless others. You are my source."

Jesus' Words that Point to this Commandment

Matthew 4:9-10, Matthew 6:24,31-33, Matthew 13:22-23, Matthew 23:25, Mark 4:19-20, Mark 10:21-24, Luke 8:14-15, Luke 12:19-21, Luke 16:19-31, Luke 18:24-25, John 6:26-29

And my God will liberally supply (fill until full) your every need according to His riches in glory in Christ Jesus. Philippians 4:19 AMP

How can I apply this to my life?

All these blessings will come upon you and overtake you if you pay attention to the voice of the Lord your God. You will be blessed in the city, and you will be blessed in the field.

Deuteronomy 28:2-3 AMP

Leave Your Past Behind.

Red Letters

And Jesus said unto him, "No man, having put his hand to the plow, and looking back, is fit for the Kingdom of God." Luke 9:62 AMP

To walk in the Kingdom of God you must look forward. When you accepted Jesus as your Savior, your sins were washed by a flood into the depths of the sea (Micah 7:19), never to be remembered again. Don't keep asking forgiveness for the past or keep looking at past hurts. Anyone who puts their hand to the plow and looks back will never get the job done. It will be a crooked mess if they do!

Ahead of you is Heaven. Within you is the Kingdom of Heaven. Behind you the past is frozen. To grow and change is to look forward, toward love. You are walking toward the ultimate victory. Keep walking and do not sit down and wallow in the fertilizer. You are now part of the overcoming life. Don't focus on the world around you and all its distractions. The mud of offense and bitterness will slow you down.

The Holy Spirit reminds us in Colossians 3:2-3 (TPT), "Christ's resurrection is your resurrection too. This is why we are to yearn [set our affections] on all that is above, for that is where Christ sits enthroned at the place of all power, honor, and authority! Yes, feast on all the treasures of the heavenly realm and fill your thoughts with heavenly realities, and not with the distractions of the natural realm. Your crucifixion with Christ has severed the tie to this life, and now your true life is hidden away in God in Christ."

Remember you do not plow this life alone. The Holy Spirit is right beside you, teaching you how to stand on the solid ground of His Word, and He will show you how to keep your eyes on the heavenly prize.

Prayer

"Lord, I turn my eyes to You. Today is the day I will leave behind unforgiveness, disappointment, condemnation and anything else that weakens me and keeps me from moving forward toward You. I am putting on my spiritual blinders and I am making a decision to firmly walk the path toward Your glory."

Jesus' Words that Point to this Commandment

Matthew 6:15, Matthew 9:2, Matthew 18:21-22, Matthew 24:13-14, Matthew 25:31-46, Luke 9:61-62, Luke 10:38-42, Luke 11:2-4

Therefore, since we are surrounded by so great a cloud of witnesses [who by faith have testified to the truth of God's absolute faithfulness], stripping off every unnecessary weight and the sin which so easily and cleverly entangles us, let us run with endurance and active persistence the race that is set before us, [looking away from all that will distract us and] focusing our eyes on Jesus, who is the Author and Perfecter of faith [the first incentive for our belief and the One who brings our faith to maturity], who for the joy [of accomplishing the goal] set before Him endured the cross, disregarding the shame, and sat down at the right hand of the throne of God [revealing His deity, His authority, and the completion of His work]. Hebrews 12:1-2 AMP

How can I apply this to my life?

____

____

____

Do Not Let the World Determine Your Success.

Red Letters

Jesus said, "Be glad and supremely joyful, for your reward in Heaven is great (strong and intense), for in this same way people persecuted the prophets who were before you."
Matthew 5:12 AMP

Worldly success is obtaining popularity or profit, and a hunger for that success is never satisfied. Jesus has a different definition of success.

When He sat His followers down and told them who is blessed in this world, it went opposite with what the world says. He said to not look at the rich and famous in this world and count them blessed. It is the poor who are blessed because they are motivated to seek God and as a result, they receive the richest kingdom, the Kingdom of God, and they are satisfied.

Likewise, it is the hungry who are blessed because they will actively seek God to fill them and they will be satisfied.

It is the sad-hearted who are blessed because they will desperately seek God and He will lead them to real joy, and they will be satisfied.

It is the ones who are rejected by the mainstream and mocked because of their Christian beliefs who will receive the highest rewards and be eternally satisfied.

See the world through Jesus' eyes. Pursue His idea of success and you will be truly satisfied.

Prayer

"Lord, pour Your love into my heart and wash away all worldly desires. Those desires toss me around and make me soulfully sick. I receive Your wealth, which is wholeness in every area of my life. Bless me, Lord."

Jesus' Words that Point to this Commandment

Matthew 5:1-12, Matthew 16:24-28, Luke 6:21-23

Jesus said, "Blessed [joyful, nourished by God's goodness] are you who hunger now [for righteousness, actively seeking right standing with God], for you will be [completely] satisfied. Blessed [forgiven, refreshed by God's grace] are you who weep now [over your sins and repent], for you will laugh [when the burden of sin is lifted]."
Luke 6:21 AMP

How can I apply this to my life?

____

____

____

____

____

____

____

____

My soul rests in God alone. My salvation come from Him. He alone is my rock and my salvation. He is my fortress. I will never be shaken.

Psalm 62:5

Take the Word of God Like a Seed and Plant It in Your Heart.

Red Letters

Jesus said, "The seed cast in the weeds represents the ones who hear the kingdom news but are overwhelmed with worries about all the things they have to do and all the things they want to get.
The stress strangles what they heard, and nothing comes of it."
Mark 4:19 MSG

When God sent Adam out of the garden, He sent him as a farmer. Even now, we are all farmers who daily plant spiritual seed. There is good spiritual seed that when cared for, creates a harvest of good things, and there is bad spiritual seed that takes root and grows a wicked harvest.

This is how you plant good spiritual seed: Find a promise of God in the scriptures. Read it. Believe it. By doing this, you have chosen good seed and prepared it for planting.

Now, speak out that promise. Read it aloud more than once a day. This is the way you begin to move the soil of your heart around, preparing a place for the seed. After reading it aloud many times, you begin to remember it by heart. This is the way the soil of your heart closes over the seed and captures the seed.

You remember that seed throughout the day and begin to thank God for the promise every time you think of it. This is the watering of that seed.

God sees the seed you planted and pays attention to His Word: "As the rain and snow come down from heaven and stay upon the ground to water the earth and cause the grain to grow and to produce seed for the

farmer and bread for the hungry, so also is My Word. I send it out, and it always produces fruit. It shall accomplish all I want it to and prosper everywhere I send it" (Isaiah 55:10-11).
God is pure light. He is the sun, warming and giving power to the seed. His Light gives life to the promise.

When that seed digs its roots into the soil of your heart and it grows into a fruit bearing tree, no one can take it from you. No circumstance can rip it from you. It becomes more real than what you see and feel. If God says it, it is true. If God promises it, it will come to pass.

But like an earthly seed, if you leave it unprotected it will be stolen away from you or choked by the weeds of worldly cares or even just shrivel up from neglect.

Prayer

"Lord, I will tend the garden of Your Word in my heart. You bless me above what I can imagine."

Jesus' Words that Point to this Commandment

Matthew 13:1-23,24-32, Matthew 17:20, Mark 4:3-20, Mark 4:26-29, Luke 8:5-15, Luke 13:18-19, John 4:35-38

> *Jesus said, "Because of your little faith," Jesus told them. "For if you had faith even as small as a tiny mustard seed, you could say to this mountain, 'Move!' and it would go far away. Nothing would be impossible." Matthew 17:20 TLB*

How can I apply this to my life?

____

____

____

____

There are Two Types of Christians: Those Who are Focused on Christianity and Those Who are Focused on Christ. Focus on Christ.

Red Letters

She had a sister, Mary, who sat before the Master, hanging on every word he said. But Martha was pulled away by all she had to do in the kitchen. Later, she stepped in, interrupting them. "Master, don't you care that my sister has abandoned the kitchen to me? Tell her to lend me a hand." The Master said, "Martha, dear Martha, you're fussing far too much and getting yourself worked up over nothing. One thing only is essential, and Mary has chosen it—it's the main course and won't be taken from her." Luke 10:40-42 MSG

Mary was listening. Martha was busy...with a good idea.
Jesus was lovingly telling Martha her investment in busily doing the work of ministry was good, but at the end of the day, when her work was done, she would be empty. The same work would need to start again the next day.

While Mary sat at her Master's feet, she was receiving truth for tomorrow. The revelations she received in His presence caused her spirit to be filled. She received strength for the journey from His Word.

This choice gave her wisdom to accomplish the next task of ministry.
The energy to carry out good ideas always wears out, but revelations from Jesus can never be taken away.

Be the one who spends time every day with Jesus. Every time you read the Word and study it, you grow up in the things of God and understand the One you serve. When you seek to understand, it will be revealed to you. When you listen, wisdom will bring balance to your life.

Weariness in doing good deeds is a sign you need to spend time with the Master. Focus on Christ and then you will be ready to serve.

Prayer

"Lord, I open my ears to Your teaching. I will not live on yesterday's revelations. Fill me today, new and afresh with Your Holy Spirit. Feed me again with Your Word."

Jesus' Words that Point to this Commandment

Matthew 4:4, Matthew 6:31-33, Matthew 7:24-25, Matthew 13:11-12, Luke 8:18, Luke 10:38-42, Luke 11:28

Jesus said, "So be careful how you listen; for whoever has, to him shall be given more; and whoever does not have, even what he thinks he has shall be taken away from him." Luke 8:18

How can I apply this to my life?

Answer this Question: Who Do You Say That I Am?

Red Letters

Jesus said to them, "But who do you say that I am?" Simon Peter replied, "You are the Christ (the Messiah, the Anointed), the Son of the living God." Matthew 16:15-16 AMP

When you answer this question, you define your faith.
It is a question Jesus is personally asking you to answer today. He doesn't want to know what you have heard or what the crowds say. Who *is* He to *you*? And He is asking you to "say" it out-loud.

We find out who He is in the living Word of God. We discover those truths as we read and then believe what is written concerning Him. We answer this question from the intimate relationship He has with us.

Continue to find out who Jesus says He is in His Word. Listen to the Holy Spirit as He reveals Jesus to you. Declare out loud who He is, as you enter His Holy Presence.

When you remind yourself of who He is, your faith will rise. Your confession of who He is causes the Kingdom of God to come near. The angels and all the citizens of Heaven wait for your answer. When you declare Him to be your Messiah, your Wonderful Counselor, your Mighty God, your Extraordinary Strategist, your Everlasting Father, your Prince of Peace (Isaiah 9:6-7), your Healer...He moves on your behalf.

The psalmist asks, "I look to the mountains, where does my help come from?" He immediately answers by saying, "My help comes from the maker of Heaven and earth!" (Psalm 121)

The more you study the Word of God and spend time with the Lord, the more you know Him. The more you know His character, the stronger your faith will become.

The relationship Jesus seeks with you is a personal one. He wants to know who YOU say He is. Don't be surprised if He responds by telling you who YOU are in Him.

Prayer

"Lord, You hold all of creation in the palm of Your hand, yet Your holy Word says Your eye is on me. Jesus told me You know everything about me. You formed me. Your plans for my life are only for good. You wait for me to choose to love You. I love You."

Jesus' Words that Point to this Commandment

Matthew 16:13-19, Matthew 22:29-32, Luke 9:13-20, John 1:1-5, John 3:14-17, John 6:29-40,68-69

Jesus said, "For God sent not his Son into the world to condemn the world; but that the world through him might be saved." John 3:17 KJV

How can I apply this to my life?

____

____

____

____

____

His name will be: The Wonderful One! The Extraordinary Strategist! The Mighty God! The Father of Eternity! The Prince of Peace! Great and vast is His dominion. Isaiah 9:6 TPT

Embrace the Weak.

Red Letters

They started arguing over which of them would be most famous. When Jesus realized how much this mattered to them, He brought a child to His side. "Whoever accepts this child as if the child were Me, accepts Me," He said. "And whoever accepts Me, accepts the One who sent Me. You become great by accepting, not asserting. Your spirit, not your size, makes the difference."

Luke 9:48 MSG

Your highest calling is to embrace the weak.

Jesus is not impressed with the beauty of your church building, the numbers of those who listen to you, or the amount of worldly honor you possess. Your greatness is found in the small moments when no one else is watching.

Jesus is there when you embrace the weak: the ones without a voice, the poor, the forgotten, and the powerless.

Power, authority and influence are worldly crowns. Meekness, humility and kindness are heavenly and eternal crowns.

Historically, the greatest witness of Christianity has been this compassion for those who are weak in the world. During the Roman plague everyone left the city except the Christians who cared for the sick and dying. The Romans had no explanation for this, and many turned to Christ.

The world will know us by our love.

Prayer

"Lord, help me see, hear and hold those who have been cast away. Today I bow my head and ask for forgiveness for exalting my own works. When I bow down to You, I can see those who are low. Show me who needs my help today."

Jesus' Words that Point to this Commandment

Matthew 10:38-42, Matthew 18:4-5, Matthew 25:31-46, Mark 9:33-37, Luke 9:46-48, Luke 14:8-14, Luke 22:25-30, John 13:31-38

> *Jesus said, "By this everyone will know that you are My disciples, if you have love and unselfish concern for one another." John 13:35 AMP*

How can I apply this to my life?

____

____

____

____

____

____

____

____

He raises up the poor from the dust; He lifts the needy from the ash heap to make them sit with princes and inherit a seat of honor. For the pillars of the earth are the Lord's, and on them He has set the world.

1 Samuel 2:8

Wisely Use Money.

Red Letters

Jesus said, "If therefore ye have not been faithful in the unrighteous mammon, who will commit to your trust the true riches?"
Luke 16:11 KJV

Money is a tool. When believers have money the world gets fed, clothed, and set free by the gospel. When evil people have money, the enemy has his way and suffering follows.

As followers of Jesus, we look to how He handled finances. Many people think Jesus lived in poverty, but He had a treasurer (John 12:6). A treasurer is needed when there are sums of money that come in and sums of money that go out.

Jesus listened to the voice of God and obeyed His commandments, so the financial blessings listed in Deuteronomy 28 surely came upon Him. He was able to go about "doing good" because He is the Healer and He had the resources to help those who were burdened.

When Judas left to betray Jesus, the other disciples thought their Master had sent him to give to the poor. Something he must have done regularly.

The Bible says, "the wealth of the sinner is laid up for the just" (Proverbs 13:22) and the "blessing of the Lord brings wealth" (Proverbs 10:22). It does not say that money is the root of all evil, but rather "The LOVE of money is the root of all kinds of evil" (1 Timothy 6:10).

Part of God's promise is to prosper you.
When you wisely handle money, others can be blessed.

You can have money, just don't let money have you.

Prayer

"Lord, give me wisdom. Help me to be wise in the area of finances and generous in my giving."

Jesus' Words that Point to this Commandment

Matthew 6:1-4, Matthew 13:44, Matthew 25:14-30, Luke 14:28-30, Luke 16:9-13

> *The Lord will open for you His good treasure house, the heavens, to give rain to your land in its season and to bless all the work of your hand; and you will lend to many nations, but you will not borrow.*
> *Deuteronomy 28:12 AMP*

How can I apply this to my life?

____

____

____

____

____

____

____

____

"Bring the whole tithe into the storehouse. Test Me in this," says the Lord Almighty, "and see if I will not throw open the floodgates of heaven and pour out so much blessing that you will not have room enough for it.

Malachi 3:10

Always Give Reverence to the Holy Spirit.

Red Letters

Jesus said, "Therefore, I tell you, every sin and blasphemy (every evil, abusive, injurious speaking, or indignity against sacred things) can be forgiven men, but blasphemy against the [Holy] Spirit shall not and cannot be forgiven." Matthew 12:3

The Holy Spirit is not a mystical force. The Holy Spirit is a person in the Godhead but without physical form on earth.
Jesus took the form of man, and the Father of lights is so powerful that men cannot stay alive in His presence (Exodus 33:20), but the person of the Holy Spirit has been given to you. He will never leave you.

His person reflects all the qualities of Christ and characteristics of God. He is the One who unveils the truth for you (John 16:13).

Jesus says, "I will ask the Father, and He will give you another Helper (Comforter, Advocate, Intercessor, Counselor, Strengthener, Standby) to be with you forever- the Spirit of Truth, whom the world cannot receive [and take to its heart] because it does not see Him or know Him, but you know Him because He (the Holy Spirit) remains with you continually and will be in you." (John 14:15-31 AMP)

Only a believer knows the Holy Spirit. Every believer who has received Jesus in their heart has been sealed by the Holy Spirit (John 20:22). It is then our responsibility to ask Him to fill us so that He can move us.

As believers we are given precious manifestations of the Holy Spirit. And each believer will receive different manifestations: "Each person is given something to do that shows who God is; wise counsel, clear understanding, simple trust, healing the sick, miraculous acts, proclamation, distinguishing between spirits, tongues and interpretation of tongues" (1 Corinthians 12:8-11 MSG).

When these gifts are in effect, always give reverence to the Holy Spirit. Don't give credit for these gifts to anyone or anything else but the Holy Spirit. Never take lightly or mock the manifestations of the Holy Spirit.

Never lessen the glory of God.

Prayer

"I welcome You, Holy Spirit, into my life. It is Your quiet voice that leads me to the left or right. Today I will be aware of Your loving leadership."

Jesus' Words that Point to this Commandment

Matthew 12:31-33, Mark 3:20-30, Luke 12:4-12, Luke 24:45-49

> *Jesus said, "You can see now how it is written that the Messiah suffers, rises from the dead on the third day, and then a total life-change through the forgiveness of sins is proclaimed in his name to all nations—starting from here, from Jerusalem! You're the first to hear and see it. You're the witnesses. What comes next is very important: I am sending what my Father promised to you, so stay here in the city until He arrives, until you're equipped with power from on high." Luke 24:49 MSG*

How can I apply this to my life?

___

___

___

___

___

Give to Those Who Can't Repay You.

Red Letters

Then Jesus turned to the host. "The next time you put on a dinner, don't just invite your friends and family and rich neighbors, the kind of people who will return the favor. Invite some people who never get invited out, the misfits from the wrong side of the tracks. You'll be—and experience—a blessing. They won't be able to return the favor, but the favor will be returned—oh, how it will be returned!—at the resurrection of God's people." Luke 14:12-14 MSG

Live a merciful life.

Pray for those who would never think to pray for you. Be a friend to those who can do nothing for you. Make dinner for a man who could never return the meal. Say a nice word about a woman you know speaks badly about you. Do a kind act and don't let anyone on social media know what you did. Send an anonymous gift to someone.

Not only do you receive a gift in your own heart for the present moment, but it will be credited to you at the resurrection. This is referring to your heavenly treasure.

When you give, and that person has no way to return the favor, they often thank God for the blessing. God is glorified and you have played a part.

Isaiah 61:3-4 speaks of the giving believer: "They will be as Mighty Oaks of Righteousness planted by Yahweh as a living display of His glory. They will restore ruins from long ago and rebuild what was long devastated... All who see them will recognize that they are the seed that Yahweh has blessed *with favor!*"

And the Holy Spirit makes this promise to you: "Let giving flow from your heart, not from a sense of religious duty. Let it spring up freely from the joy of giving...Yes! God is more than ready to overwhelm you with every form of grace, so that you will have more than enough of everything-every moment and in every way. He will make you overflow with abundance in every good thing you do" (2 Corinthians 9:7-8 TPT).

Prayer

"Lord, I am unworthy to receive Your righteousness, Your holiness, or Your perfection on me. These are all part of Your free gift to me through the works of Jesus. You did not give me what I deserved, so help me not give people what they deserve. I want to always give through Your unselfish love."

Jesus' Words that Point to this Commandment

Matthew 25:35-40, Luke 6:27-38, Luke 14:12-24, Luke 15:11-24, Luke 16:9

Jesus said, "It is important to use the wealth of this world to demonstrate your friendship with God by winning friends and blessing others. Then, when this world fails and falls apart, your generosity will provide you with an eternal reward." Luke 16:9

How can I apply this to my life?

____

____

____

____

____

____

Do Not Think Too Highly of Yourself.

Red Letters

But Jesus said to them, "You are the ones who declare yourselves just and upright before men, but God knows your hearts. For what is exalted and highly thought of among men is detestable and abhorrent (an abomination) in the sight of God." Luke 16:15 AMP

Our Christian walk began with the words, "Forgive me, Father. I am a sinner." As you grow up in Christ never let pride replace the tenderness of a repentant heart.

You can make yourself look good in the sight of other people, but God knows your heart. Every truly good thing you do comes from a close relationship with your Heavenly Father, who is good and perfect. When you yield to Him, you reflect His goodness, not your own.

Know that if you are dishonest in a small, unseen act, you will be dishonest in a larger one. What is in the dark will always be brought in the light...this goes for the good and the bad. (Mark 4:22)

Walk your Christianity out in secret as well as out in the open. Remember, what the world says is success is often shameful in the sight of God. Surrender any envy and any pursuit of worldly honor.
These things will hinder your walk with God and steal your peace.

And remember to not fall into a false humility, which is also pride. "True Humility is not thinking less of yourself, it's thinking of yourself less" (C.S. Lewis, Mere Christianity).

Prayer

"Lord, place Your yoke on my shoulders. It is a yoke of love for others. I will let it define me. I repent of exalting my needs above others."

Jesus' Words that Point to this Commandment

Matthew 5:3-16, Matthew 11:28-30, Matthew 12:35-37, Matthew 15:4-8, Luke 6:23-26

> *Jesus said, "Learn my ways and you'll discover that I am gentle, humble, easy to please. You will find refreshment and rest in Me. For all that I require of you will be pleasant and easy to bear."*
> *Luke 16:9-10 TPT*

How can I apply this to my life?

____

____

____

____

____

____

____

____

____

____

____

Humble yourselves before the Lord, and He will lift you up.

James 4:10

Red Letters

But the centurion replied to Him, Lord, I am not worthy or fit to have You come under my roof; but only speak the word, and my servant boy will be cured. For I also am a man subject to authority, with soldiers subject to me. And I say to one, Go, and he goes; and to another, Come, and he comes; and to my slave, 'Do this', and he does it. When Jesus heard him, He marveled and said to those who followed Him, "I tell you truly, I have not found so much faith as this with anyone, even in Israel."
Matthew 8:5-10 AMP

What would you think of a man who had a willing servant but did all the work himself?

The centurion saw faith like a servant. Spoken out of the mouth of authority, faith can be sent to accomplish its task. Jesus was pleased with the centurion's attitude toward faith.

Let's study this attitude so we can respond the same way.
The centurion understood who had authority over him. He also knew who and what he himself had authority over. He lived and worked by the principles of authority. He perceived that Jesus had great authority and that authority was released through the Words of Jesus, so he responded to the problem by saying, "Just say the WORD, and my servant will be healed."

You are also subject to an authority. That authority is the Word of God. When you submit yourself to the Word and then speak it over your life, you allow that authority to take over your circumstances. When you speak the Word of God, you are speaking with the same authority Jesus had to heal the servant of the centurion. Jesus is the Living Word (John 1:14).

Once you step into this doubt-free mindset of authority, you will speak in faith just as Jesus taught you: "You shall say to this mountain, be thou removed and cast into the sea and it will be done." (Matthew 21:21 KJV)

Now go and activate your faith. We declare His promises over our lives in faith and that faith moves circumstances on this earth. Speak His promises of healing, protection, provision, and salvation over your life. Believe His WORD has authority. Impress Jesus with your faith.

Prayer

"Lord, thank you for the authority of Your Word. When I speak Your Word over my life, it takes control. I make a decision today, like the centurion, to believe all the promises of life You have for me and my household, regardless of what I see."

Jesus' Words that Point to this Commandment

Matthew 8:5-13, Matthew 21:21-22, Mark 5:25-34, Luke 17:6-9

> *"If your faith were only the size of a mustard seed," Jesus answered, "it would be large enough to uproot that mulberry tree over there and send it hurtling into the sea! Your command would bring immediate results!" Luke 17:6 TLB*

How can I apply this to my life?

____

____

____

____

____

Discard Your Religious Traditions. I Am the Rock That Supports All That You Believe.

Red Letters

Jesus said, "Read it for yourself in your Bibles: 'The stone the masons threw out is now the cornerstone. This is God's work; we rub our eyes, we can hardly believe it!'
This is the way it is with you. God's kingdom will be taken back from you and handed over to a people who will live out a kingdom life. Whoever stumbles on this Stone gets shattered; whoever the Stone falls on gets smashed." Matthew 21:42-44 MSG

The word "religion" has been used in place of "faith" or "belief system". This is incorrect. Religion is man-made and those that follow it obey rules of conduct designed by its founders. Those rules make a person holy in the sight of man. Religion consists of performing ancient traditions and rituals in a public way. Religion is a label for a person to cover themselves.

Relationship with Jesus breaks apart from every idea of "holiness" religion offers: "For God made the only one who did not know sin to become sin for us, so that we, who do not know righteousness might become the righteousness of God through our union with Him (2 Corinthians 5:21 TPT). A divine exchange happened on the cross of Jesus Christ. All our sins were left there. All our guilt was left there. We walk away with ALL of God's righteousness. When we simply believe in Jesus Christ, we are seen by the One True God, our Creator, as righteous as His sinless Son! He is asking for our faith, not religion.

In Christ you are in relationship. The religious traditions of men have no place in "relationship" with Christ. Jesus teaches us, very clearly, that the religious traditions men create will weaken the power of the Word of God, His Word, in your life (Mark 7 :13).

In the end it comes down to this: Some will fall at the feet of Jesus and their sin will be broken, others will reject Jesus, claiming their own holiness, and the stone of judgement will fall on them. Don't be deceived. Everything God has built began with Jesus, is upheld by Jesus, and ends with Jesus.

Prayer

"Lord, You are my Rock. You have crushed the sin that would have pulled me under to my death. You have put me in a high place, on a strong foundation, and I will be there for eternity. I worship You and honor You. You are my Salvation!"

Jesus' Words that Point to this Commandment

Matthew 21:42-44, Mark 7:13, Mark 12:10-11, Luke 20:17-18, John 1:1-5, John 14:6-14

> *Jesus replied, "How accurately did Isaiah prophesy about you phonies when he said, 'These people honor Me with their words while their hearts run far-away from Me! Their worship is nothing more than a charade! For they continue to insist that their man-made traditions are equal to the instructions of God.' You abandon God's commandments just to keep men's rituals..." Mark 7:6-8 TPT*

How can I apply this to my life?

____

____

____

____

____

Red Letters

Jesus said, "But take heed to yourselves and be on your guard, lest your hearts be overburdened and depressed (weighed down) with the giddiness and headache and nausea of self-indulgence, drunkenness, and worldly worries and cares pertaining to [the business of] this life, and [lest] that day come upon you suddenly like a trap or a noose; For it will come upon all who live upon the face of the entire earth."

Luke 21:34-36 AMP

If you indulge yourself too much and let your heart get depressed and filled with worldly worries and cares, you will be weighted to this world and the day of the Lord will catch you off guard.

Always be prepared and be awake in the spirit! Do not be a flesh-centered (a body-focused and reasoning-focused) Christian. Be a spirit-centered Christian who listens to the Holy Spirit and yields to Him.

If something starts to weigh you down, get alone with the Lord. Grief is heavy. Sin is heavy. Anxiety and depression are heavy. Fear is heavy. But Isaiah 10:27 (TPT) says that the Lord Yahweh will "remove the heavy burden from your shoulders and break off the yoke of bondage from your necks because of the heavy anointing on you!" Believer, *YOU* need to release it.

He will comfort you and turn you in the right direction. Repent, get focused again, find the powerful anointing of joy, and stand up.

Get "heavy" with the Word of God. It stands forever here on earth and in heaven.

Pray that you have the full strength and ability (given by the Holy Spirit) to be accounted worthy to stand in the presence of the Son of God on that great day.
Be ready to go wholeheartedly in the Spirit with no ties to the earth.

Prayer

"Lord, I lay down at Your feet worry, grief, fear, frustration, and any other weighty thing on my heart. Cleanse me of negative thinking while I read Your life-giving Word. You are my hope. You are my future. You are my Lord. Come, Lord Jesus, come!"

Jesus' Words that Point to this Commandment

Matthew 11:28, Matthew 24:42-51, Mark 4:19, Luke 10:38-42, Luke 12:40-48, Luke 21:19,33-36

> *Jesus replied, "You too, be continually ready; because the Son of Man is coming at an hour that you do not expect." Luke 12:40 AMP*

How can I apply this to my life?

____

____

____

____

____

____

Here's what I have learned through it all: Don't give up; don't be impatient; be entwined as one with the Lord. Be brave and courageous and never lose hope. Yes, keep on waiting- for He will never disappoint you. Psalm 27:14 TPT

Do Not Cry Because of My Crucifixion.
Cry for Those Who Do Not Know Me as Their Savior.

Red Letters

Following Jesus was a large crowd of the people, including women who were mourning and wailing for Him. But Jesus, turning toward them, said, "Daughters of Jerusalem, do not weep for Me, but weep for yourselves and for your children."
Luke 23:27-28 AMP

There was a price that had to be paid for your sin. It could not be paid by good works. It could not be paid with financial offerings. Every human has a stain that could only be washed clean by the blood shed on the cross by a sinless human. Jesus paid that price.

It was a cost that He and His Father incurred for you. Your only responsibility is to believe. The only work that is required of you is to believe.

One of the most powerful questions you can ask the Lord is, "Why the cross?" If you are sincere and ready to hear, He will unfold revelation into your heart, so you can understand.

He made an investment that cost Him greatly. His inheritance is your heart. His inheritance is to hold you close and call you "My beloved child!"

When you find yourself pained by what He had to go through as punishment for your sin, turn your passion toward those who need the cross.

This is what you can do for Jesus.

Prayer

"Lord, thank you for the cross. You had a choice. When You allowed Yourself to be placed there, You took my place. You bore my grief, sorrow, sin, sickness and disease. As a result, I am healed. Help me with boldness to draw others to Your healing."

Jesus' Words that Point to this Commandment

Matthew 9:37-38, Matthew 28:19-20, Mark 16:15-16, Luke 19:9-10, Luke 23:28-31, John 1:9-13, John 3:16-21, John 10:9-11

> *Jesus said, "He who believes [who adheres to and trusts in and relies on the Gospel and Him Whom it sets forth] and is baptized will be saved from the penalty of eternal death; but he who does not believe [who does not adhere to and trust in and rely on the Gospel and Him Whom it sets forth] will be condemned." Mark 16:16 AMP*

How can I apply this to my life?

____

____

____

____

____

____

____

____

Jesus said to him, "I am the way, and the truth, and the life. No one comes to the Father except through Me." John 14:6

Do Not Wait to Share the Gospel with Someone.

Red Letters

Jesus said, "Do you think the work of harvesting will not begin until the summer ends four months from now? Look around you! Vast fields of human souls are ripening all around us and are ready now for reaping."
John 4:35 TLB

Fear of failure. Fear of rejection. Fear of not knowing enough. Fear that you are not the perfect Christian. Everyone who shares the gospel has to overcome these fears. Get over it. The time is now.

It is really easy work. You don't need to research every argument or study every religion to be an evangelist. You just need to be able to share what God has done for you.

You do not need to be perfect, actually it is better if you aren't.

Jesus has done the hard part. Your part is to just lead them to Him.
It is not your job to convince them, that is the Holy Spirit's part. It is not your words that save people. Revelation of who Jesus is will save them.

He needs you to step up and do your part to show them the door.
Your paycheck will be eternal joy.
Try to beat that.

Prayer
"Lord, I lay at Your feet any fear I have of people. I receive Your perfect love overwhelming my heart and uprooting that fear. I will share that love today. Help me see my life with an eternal perspective"

Jesus' Words that Point to this Commandment

Matthew 4:19-22, Matthew 9:35-38, Mark 4:25-29, Mark 8:35, Mark 13:10-11, Luke 10:2-16, John 4:35-38, John 14:27

Jesus called out, "Come along with me and I will show you how to fish for the souls of men!" Matthew 4:19 TLB

How can I apply this to my life?

____

____

____

____

____

____

____

____

____

____

He has enough treasures to lavish generously upon all who call on Him. And it's true: "Everyone who calls on the name of the Lord will be rescued and experience new life." But how can people call on Him for help if they've not yet believed? And how can they believe in One they've not yet heard of? And how can they hear the message of life if there is no one there to proclaim it? And how can the message be proclaimed if messengers have yet to be sent? That's why the scriptures say: "How welcome is the arrival of those proclaiming the joyful news of peace and the good things to come!" Romans 10:13-15 TPT

Move Forward Healed.

Red Letters

Jesus said, "Pick up your stretcher and go on home, for you are healed!" The man jumped up, took the stretcher, and pushed his way through the stunned onlookers! Then how they praised God. "We've never seen anything like this before!" they all exclaimed.

Mark 2:11-12 TLB

"Pick up!" "Rise!" "Go!"

These are a few of the commands Jesus gave the sick while He walked the earth. He never said, "Watch your problem, and when it goes away, be on your way." When Jesus healed, He would often follow it with a command to move forward in that healing.

What situation has you locked in like being strapped to a stretcher? Jesus paid for you to be free.

Release your problem, sickness, and weakness. Leave it behind and take that step forward.

But that means you need to stop saying to everyone, "I have this condition or that disease." He will is to heal you, but if you stay in the mindset of sickness, you will stay sick. Be ready to leave your "bed" and walk away healed.

Hear Jesus' word, believe it, and act on it. While you are at it, leave behind your expectation on how you will receive your miracle.

He is doing a new thing.

Prayer

"Lord, You are my healer. Your Word says You desire shalom, perfect wholeness, over my life. (3 John:2) You heal my mind, my heart, and my body. You go into my future to prepare the way, and in kindness you follow behind me to spare me from the harm of my past. You have laid your hand on me! (Psalm 139:5-6) I receive Your healing for me today and I move forward healed."

Jesus' Words that Point to this Commandment

Matthew 8:5-13, Matthew 9:1-8, Matthew 9:35, Mark 2:1-12, Mark 5:25-34, Luke 5:17-26, Luke 8:49-55, Luke 17:14, John 5:8-9, John 10:9-10

> *When Jesus saw them, He said to them, "Go and show yourselves to the priests." And as they went, they were [miraculously] healed and made clean. Luke 17:14 AMP*

How can I apply this to my life?

____

____

____

____

____

____

____

This is what the Lord, the God of your father David, says:

"I have heard your prayer and seen your tears; I will heal you.

2 Kings 20:5

Remember What the Lord Has Done.

Red Letters

A little later Jesus found him in the Temple and said, "You look wonderful! You're well! Don't return to a sinning life or something worse might happen." John 5:14 MSG

Remember what Jesus has done for you.

Keep a journal and write down all those answered prayers. Read them often. Psalm 103:2 says, "Don't forget all His benefits." Share them with your family and friends. Keep them before you. Read them every Sunday.

As the sun rises and sets, your life will continue to serve you challenges. Jesus will be there for you through each of them. Don't become accustomed to the blessings you receive. Count them often.

Remember the valleys of darkness He has drawn you out of. Remember how destructive sin can be. In John 5:14, Jesus is telling this man who received so much from Him, "Do not sin and don't forget My love." When we forget what He has done, we start to take credit, and this leads to pride.
Pride leads to doubt, which always leads to sin.

Jesus is saying this to protect us. A terrible thing can come on someone through willful disobedience or sin, not because God is the punisher, but because they will get themselves into a painful trap.

If Jesus has come into your life and ministered healing to you, never return to the place that hurt you. Walk away.

Prayer

"Lord, bless Your holy name. I remember all You have done for me. You have taken me out of the world of darkness and into Your loving Presence. I will not return to the darkness. I will love You and follow You all of my days."

Jesus' Words that Point to this Commandment

Matthew 12:43-45, Luke 11:24-26, Luke 22:19, John 5:14, John 14:26

> *Make sure that when you eat and are satisfied, build pleasant houses and settle in, see your herds and flocks flourish and more and more money come in, watch your standard of living going up and up—make sure you don't become so full of yourself and your things that you forget God.*
>
> *Deuteronomy 8:11-16 MSG*

How can I apply this to my life?

____

____

____

____

____

____

____

____

____

____

____

____

Desire to Do God's Will.

Red Letters

Follow Me in this:

Jesus said, "I do not seek or consult My own will. I have no desire to do what is pleasing to Myself, My own aim, My own purpose, but only the will and pleasure of the Father Who sent Me." John 5:30 AMP

Most people have a strong will and that's not a bad thing. But like a roaring flood, it can do harm or be harnessed for good.
Don't have a strong will apart from God - have a strong desire to do His will.

But how do we know what is God's will?

We hear our Saviors voice as He teaches us to pray, "Father, let Your will be done on earth as it is in heaven." What is in heaven *IS* His will on earth.

Heaven is where the glory of God shines like the sun. Do what glorifies Him. In heaven there is no shadow of sin or evil. Leave behind the self-gratifying life. In heaven the love of God is present in every way. When you focus on the truth that God loves you and you are valuable, you are free to love others. When love is your focus, you are in the will of God.

The Word of God is heaven's atmosphere. God's will is echoed in His Word. Be a person who meditates on the Word of God and allow it to govern your life choices. Your life will be like heaven on earth.

Jesus says, "I do what the Father tells me to do. I do what I see the Father do. Nothing else interests me because He is the source of my strength, wisdom, and knowledge. He is my present and future. I operate in His love." Follow Jesus as He follows the Father and you will find yourself in the center of a blessed life.

When we follow our own will, we find ourselves in the center of trouble. The search for satisfaction without God is endless.

Prayer

"Lord, I don't seek my own will, but I seek Your will in my life. I want to glorify Your Name in my life. I want others to see You when they see me."

Jesus' Words that Point to this Commandment

Matthew 6:10, Matthew 6:33, Luke 9:23-26, John 5:19-23, John 5:30,36, John 7:16-18, John 8:49-51

> *Jesus said, "[Pray like this,] Thy kingdom come, Thy will be done in earth, as it is in heaven."*
> *Matthew 6:10 KJV*

How can I apply this to my life?

____

____

____

____

____

____

____

____

Bring Me Your Seed.

Red Letters

"Then Jesus told the people to sit down on the grass, and He took the five loaves and two fish, looked up into the sky, and asked God's blessing on the meal, then broke the loaves apart and gave them to the disciples to place before the people." Matthew 14:19 TLB

How did five simple loaves of bread and two small fish feed a multitude? Our human reasoning says this is impossible. The natural and physical laws of science say, within those time parameters, it is impossible. But what if another law was at work here?
The law is a spiritual law of seedtime and harvest.

God created natural laws as patterns for things found in the spiritual realm. In the spiritual law of seedtime and harvest, the desired results are seeded in the spirit realm and harvested in the physical realm, free from the confines of time.

The boy's seed (his food) was planted with faith into the hands of Jesus. It wasn't his excess. It was his all. There was no fear in his giving.

Jesus needed that seed to perform the miracle. Jesus received it and the natural process of seed, to plant, to tree, to harvest, gave way to a heavenly (instantaneous) timing.

We must always remember that the constraint of time we as humans live by does not limit God.

He increased the bread and fish to feed them all and the leftovers were a harvest to the boy. God was glorified. People were fed. The boy was blessed.

When God blesses, He blesses in multiples. This is the law of seedtime and harvest in action. What seed does the Lord need you to plant today so others will be "fed"?

Prayer

"Lord, I give to You my seed. I release it to You, and I will not be afraid. Take it, multiply it, and bless people with it. I am joyfully expecting Your riches and glory over my life."

Jesus' Words that Point to this Commandment

Matthew 13:23, Matthew 14:16-21, Matthew 15:34-39, Mark 4:26-29, Mark 6:37-44, Luke 6:38, Luke 9:13-17, John 6:3-13

> *Jesus said, "God's kingdom realm is like someone spreading seed on the ground. He goes to bed and gets up, day after day, and the seed sprouts and grows tall, though he knows not how. All by itself it sprouts, and the soil produces a crop..." Mark 4:26-28 TPT*

How can I apply this to my life?

____

____

____

____

____

____

____

____

Do Not Be Afraid. I Will Do Things That Are Unexpected.

Red Letters

The disciples had rowed about halfway across the lake when, all of a sudden, they caught sight of Jesus walking on top of the waves, coming toward them. The disciples panicked but Jesus called to them, "Don't be afraid. You know who I am."

John 6:20 TPT

Being a follower of Jesus means you need to be ready for an adventure! Be ready for Him to do a brand-new thing. Don't put into a box all the things God can do for you. Your mind is not His boundary.

He is ready to bless your plans, but always be ready to ask, "What are your plans for me today, Lord?" You are born of God. Position your heart toward Him with expectation. Expect to be a part of things that defy natural law.

God says in Isaiah 55:8-9 (MSG), "For as the sky soars high above earth, so the way I work surpasses the way you work, and the way I think is beyond the way you think."

When the sea rose up dangerously in front of the apostles as they crossed it in a small boat, they probably prayed for the Lord to calm the waves. Instead, He walked toward them, defying the power of those deep waters, and walked *ON* them.

God created it all. He can alter what He created to make a way for answered prayer.

You are His child. Enjoy the limitless power and possibility of your Father.

Prayer

"Lord, I lay down every expectation on how You will answer my prayers. I will focus on Your ability to make a way where there seems to be no way. You are God over what man says is impossible."

Jesus' Words that Point to this Commandment

Matthew 14:27-33, Matthew 17:1-9, Mark 6:45-52, John 6:16-21

> *"Be alert, be present. I'm about to do something brand-new. It's bursting out! Don't you see it?" Isaiah 43:19-21 MSG*

How can I apply this to my life?

For I know the plans I have for you, declares the Lord, plans for welfare and not for evil, to give you a future and a hope. Jeremiah 29:11

Don't Let Pride Trap You.

Red Letters

Follow Me in this:

All the people were astounded as they saw with their own eyes the miracle Jesus had performed! They began to say among themselves, "He really is the One-the true prophet we have been expecting. So, Jesus knowing they were about to take Him and make Him king, quickly left and went up to the mountainside alone." John 6:14-15 TPT

And when he had sent them away, he departed into a mountain to pray. Mark 6:46 KJV

After one of His greatest miracles (feeding over 5,000 people with only five loaves of bread and two fish) the people were ready to make Jesus an earthly king. He left their compliments and praises, got alone, and prayed.

This was the key to what happened next.

He then met the disciples, mid-sea, by walking on water. He entered their boat and caused time to collapse, resulting in the boat immediately arriving at the other shore (John 6:21).

Jesus' prayer kept Him focused and moving toward God's plan. Remember this when people praise you, exalt you, and lift you up. Instead of agreeing with them, remove yourself from their accolades, get alone with God, get focused, and pray.

Pride is a silent and enticing trap. Your abilities and accomplishments begin to define you, separate you, and lift you up. Like a person walking on stilts, you will find yourself alone. You will respect your way above anyone else's, your trust will begin to point to your own understanding, and it will all result in a terrible fall.

The most serious consequence of pride is it can cloud your ability to hear God. Prayer will ground you and keep you focused on God's plan and His will for your life.

Prayer will empower you, where pride will weaken you. Prayer moves you into the things of God.

Prayer

"Lord, in addition to my weaknesses and needs, I lay my abilities and strengths at Your throne. My desire is not to be flattered by men and women, but I want to hear from You: 'Well done'. Lord, show me where I go next."

Jesus' Words that Point to this Commandment

Matthew 14:22-36, Mark 6:46, Luke 1:51-52, John 6:14-21, John 17:13-19

> *(Mary's prophetic song as she was filled with the good news of her pregnancy with Jesus) "Mighty power flows from Him to scatter all those who walk in pride. Powerful princes He tears from their thrones and He lifts up the lowly to take their place. Those who hunger for Him will always be filled, but the smug and self-satisfied He will send away empty." Luke 1:51-53 TPT*

How can I apply this to my life?

____

____

____

____

____

____

Be Hungry for Things That Sustain You Eternally.

Red Letters

Jesus said, "But you shouldn't be so concerned about perishable things like food. No, spend your energy seeking the eternal life that I, the Messiah, can give you. For God the Father has sent me for this very purpose." John 6:27 TLB

A better view, a better vacation, a better office, a better title, a better body...like a sand castle made by the hands of children, when the wave comes it will all disappear. You can't take any of these things into eternal life.

Jesus is saying, "Be smart, make an eternal investment with your time on earth." Build a treasure with time spent with God.

Jesus knows you need water, food, money etc. to live on this earth. But He reminds us these are perishable. Our earthly desires and hunger will always leave us wanting more.

He paid a price for you to have perfect fellowship with the Father. When you make time to seek God's truth in the Word and spend time in prayer, hungry for His presence, you will be eternally filled.

There is Heavenly Bread available for your spirit. Jesus calls Himself "The Bread of Life" and His words are the Bread that leaves you satisfied, forever. He also offers you "living water". Jesus said, "If you drink from Jacob's well you'll be thirsty again and again, but if anyone drinks the living water I will give them, they will never thirst and be forever satisfied!" (John 4:13).

Your natural body will never be "forever satisfied". Only Jesus can provide this continual feast of truth and joy to our spirit. Our spirit is who we are for eternity.

Remember, you are a spirit who has a soul (mind, will, and emotions) and you live in a body. Your spirit *must* be fed to be well in your soul and body.

Prayer

"Lord, fill me with Your living Word. Show me why I seek anything that is not eternal. Heal me. Give me Your eternal Bread of Life and Living Water."

Jesus' Words that Point to this Commandment

Matthew 5:6, Luke 10:38-42, John 4:13-14, John 6:26-35,58, John 10:27-29

> *Jesus said, "Yes, I am the Bread of Life! When your fathers in the wilderness ate bread from the skies, they all died. But the Bread from heaven gives eternal life to everyone who eats it. I am that Living Bread that came down out of heaven. Anyone eating this Bread shall live forever; this Bread is my flesh given to redeem humanity."*
>
> *John 6:48-51 TLB*

How can I apply this to my life?

____

____

____

____

____

____

____

Believe Me.

Red Letters

Jesus said, "The work of God is this: to believe in the One He has sent."
John 6:29

During Jesus' three-year ministry on earth He spoke over eighty times about believing. He said, "You believe in God, believe in Me", "Believe Me, that I am in the Father", "Do you believe in the Son of God?", "Believe Me", "Do you believe Me now?", "Don't be afraid, only believe", and many more.

You have a heart within you that is designed to believe. You are always believing something. Jesus' invitation to the world is to set their believing heart on Him. The Kingdom of God is only entered through the door of believing Jesus. Believing Jesus connects you to eternal life.

He said "I am the Resurrection and the Life...anyone who clings to Me in faith, even though he dies will live forever. And the one who lives by believing in Me will never die. Do you believe this?" (John 11:25-26).

All of eternity waits for your answer.

And always remember that we keep believing. This is our "work" on earth (John 6:29). We need to be diligent to attach our believing heart to the promises found in God's Word.

Religious pressure has made people believe it is their good works that make them worthy of heaven, but Jesus said, it is believing.

The Holy Spirit reminds us in Romans 10:10-11, "The heart that believes in Him receives the gift of the righteousness of God...Everyone who believes in Him will never be disappointed."

Prayer

"Jesus, I choose to believe You are the Son of God. I believe You are the gift of eternal life given to me from the Father. I believe."

Jesus' Words that Point to this Commandment

Matthew 7:13-14, Mark 1:15-18, John 6:66-68, John 10:27-28, 37-42

> *Jesus said, "Enter through the narrow gate. For wide is the gate and broad and easy to travel is the path that leads the way to destruction and eternal loss, and there are many who enter through it. But small is the gate and narrow and difficult to travel is the path that leads the way to [everlasting] life, and there are few who find it." Matthew 7:13-14 AMP*

How can I apply this to my life?

____

____

____

____

____

____

____

____

And without faith it is impossible to please God, because anyone who comes to Him must believe that He exists and that He rewards those who earnestly seek Him. Hebrews 11:6

Be Compassionate. Love Without Condemnation.

Red Letters

Follow Me in this:

Jesus was left alone, with the woman standing there before Him in the center of the court. When Jesus raised Himself up, He said to her, "Woman, where are your accusers? Has no man condemned you?" She answered, No one, Lord! And Jesus said, "I do not condemn you either. Go on your way and from now on sin no more." John 8:10-11 AMP

Compassion, mercy, and kindness are what changes the heart of a person. Your judgement or condemnation doesn't stop them from sinning. It never has.

Jesus' attitude toward this woman caught in adultery was not to separate Himself from her with condemnation, but to embrace her with compassion. He encouraged her with His forgiveness and gave her hope for a new life.

"We must learn to regard people less in the light of what they do or omit to do, and more in the light of what they suffer." -Dietrich Bonhoeffer

Those who sin need a Savior, not more self-control. Jesus reminds us repeatedly that a loving response is always the answer: "Love the Lord God with all of your heart, and with all your soul, and with all your mind. This is the first and greatest commandment. And the second is like it: Love your neighbor as yourself" (Matthew 22:37-39).

Provide a meal, an embrace, a kind word and show them who Jesus really is. Yield to His heart, follow Him, and walk in mercy, gentle wisdom, and grace.

Prayer

"Lord, fill me. Heal my heart so I can operate at all times in Your love."

Jesus' Words that Point to this Commandment

Matthew 5:1-12, Matthew 9:35-38, Mark 5:30-34, Luke 4:16-21, John 8:3-11, John 9:3, John 13:34-35, John 15:12-13

When He saw the crowds, He was moved with compassion and pity for them, because they were dispirited and distressed, like sheep without a shepherd. Matthew 9:36 AMP

How can I apply this to my life?

Praise be to the God and Father of our Lord Jesus Christ, the Father of compassion and the God of all comfort, who comforts us in all our troubles, so that we can comfort those in any trouble with the comfort we ourselves receive from God. 2 Corinthians 1:3-4

Love Each Other.

Red Letters

Jesus said, "I give you a new commandment: that you should love one another. Just as I have loved you, so you too should love one another."
John 13:34 AMP

"I love you." Maybe you have said this to your parents or a sibling. Maybe to a spouse or boyfriend or girlfriend. It means different things to different people. Some people say they "love" a restaurant or a song. Some people "love" the beach or a beautiful sunset.

In English we have one word for love. In Greek and Hebrew, the original languages of the Bible, there are many words for love. There are words for romantic love, brotherly love, love for an object, spontaneous love, a devoted love, etc. The type of love Jesus walked in and commands us to walk in is called "agape" love.

Agape love is not based on the worth of an object. It is a chosen love. It is unconditional and does not change if the person is unlovable, unkind, or unworthy. It is a consuming passion for the well-being of others. Agape love delights in giving.

This is a God kind of love. It is the kind of love Jesus has toward you and it is the love that was planted in your heart when you became a child of God (Romans 5:5). It is a love you do on purpose. Everything you do in this life should be founded in this love. The world will know you by this love.

This is what practicing agape love looks like: You will weep with others.

You will respond to bad behavior with mercy. You will believe in new beginnings for people. You will teach with patience. You will desire to feed those who are physically and spiritually hungry. You will want to heal. You will pray for others with the same passion you pray for yourself. You will give up your plan and do what you can to help others. You will love those who hate you.

You will resist fear. You will sacrifice. You will trust God.

Prayer

"Lord, wash my mind with Your love today. Speak to my heart about this agape love and teach me how to think, speak and act by this heavenly love."

Jesus' Words that Point to this Commandment

Mark 12:31, Luke 6:35-38, John 3:16, John 13:34-35, John 15:9-17

> *Jesus said, "And here is how to measure it—the greatest love is shown when a person lays down his life for his friends." John 15:13 TLB*

How can I apply this to my life?

Your Salvation is Secure by Believing in Me. Do Not Doubt That.

Red Letters

Jesus said, "I say emphatically that anyone who listens to my message and believes in God who sent me, has eternal life, and will never be damned for his sins, but has already passed out of death into life."
John 5:24 TLB

Another translation says He says this "very seriously" to His followers. I imagine He looked His friends in the eye and made sure they understood every word He was saying. Why?

First of all, this was a major mind-shift from their religious upbringing of following the letter of the law. Jesus was revealing their gift of righteousness through faith in Him. And secondly, when Jesus left them to take His seat in Heaven, He knew they would be challenged with doubt. He wanted to make sure this truth was rooted in their heart.

He is commanding you through His word to also let this truth take root in your heart. Nothing in this world can separate you from God's promise of salvation after you have received it. Your disobedience doesn't separate you from the promise. One prayer of repentance puts you back on the path of blessing.

You do not need to pay a price. He paid it. You do not need to be perfect. He is.

By believing in the words Jesus has spoken, you have entered into His covenant with the Father. If you have entered in, you have gained salvation.

Walk in a manner worthy of His amazing love for you, but do not be deceived into believing your promise of Heaven is based on deeds.
If you listen to Jesus and believe in God who sent Him, you have already been saved.

Your name is sealed.

Prayer

"Thank you, Lord, for Your free gift of eternal life. Thank you that my destination is set. I am Yours and You are mine. Reveal to me new revelations of Your gift of righteousness."

Jesus' Words that Point to this Commandment

Matthew 7:13-14, Mark 16:16, Luke 8:21, Luke 18:27, Luke 19:10, John 5:24-25, John 8:31-36, John 14:23-24

> *For by grace are ye saved through faith; and that not of yourselves: it is the gift of God. Ephesians 2:8 KJV*

How can I apply this to my life?

___

___

___

___

___

___

___

___

___

___

Never Believe I Am the Source of Your Suffering.

Red Letters

Jesus said, "The thief's purpose is to steal, kill, and destroy. My purpose is to give life in all its fullness." John 10:10 TLB

Jesus makes this very clear. If you are confused about who is the source of your problems, remember: The thief's job (the devil) is to: 1. Steal, 2. Kill, and 3. Destroy. Jesus' job is to come and give you an abundant life.

There is an enemy of God and He is a deceiver. He has sown lies into the hearts of men since the beginning of time.

Jesus does not take your loved one to Heaven because He needs them. Jesus does not steal your dream and replace it with His plans. Jesus does not destroy whole cities with devastation to get their attention. He didn't do any of these things when He walked the earth and He isn't doing it now (Hebrews 13:8).

God does desire you to walk in the joy and blessing of His Son. He is a good Father and desires only very good things for you (James 1:17).

To walk with God you must put to death the world in you - this can be suffering for some. But He is not its source.

Your life is a precious gift from Him and He wants to guide you every day into sound thinking and abundance.

Prayer

"Lord, You are a good Father. Every good and perfect gift comes from You. Jesus, I receive the life of abundance You have promised me. You have overcome the world."

Jesus' Words that Point to this Commandment

Matthew 6:33, Matthew 7:11, Matthew 20:28, John 3:17, Luke 19:10, John 6:33, John 10:1-5, John 10:10-11, John 12:47

> *Jesus said, "The true Bread is a Person—the one sent by God from heaven, and he gives life to the world." John 6:33 TLB*

How can I apply this to my life?

____

____

____

____

____

____

____

____

____

____

____

Every good and perfect gift is from above, coming down from the Father of heavenly lights, who does not change like shifting shadows.

James 1:17

Share the Word, Not Your Advice, With Others.

Red Letters

Follow Me in this:

"For these are not my own ideas, but I have told you what the Father said to tell you. And I know his instructions lead to eternal life; so whatever he tells me to say, I say!"

John 12:49-50 TLB

Giving good advice is satisfying, but your understanding may not be enough. Your wisdom is good, but God's wisdom, through His Word, is "alive and active" (Hebrews 4:12). His wisdom will speak directly to the heart of the hearer.

Follow Jesus and say what the Father says.
Jesus told people what He heard from the Father and as a result, brought the Light of Heaven wherever He walked.

Pointing a friend to Jesus is the greatest thing you can do for them. Our hearts want to give them a quick solution, but the heart of the Holy Spirit wants to heal their deepest pain. He can deliver, heal, and restore. His touch brings a supernatural life change.

Learn what the Word says, memorize it, and share it with those that are hurting. His Word will give order to a confusing situation and healing to a painful one. It is alive and powerful and can set in motion the victory that is needed.

Make sure "His Word is near you, even in your mouth and in your heart" (Romans 10:8). His Word will bring life and dispel darkness in your own life and to those around you.

Prayer

"Lord, Your Word is alive when I speak it and it is a sword. It will get to the heart of the matter. I will not be afraid of sounding too "religious". Help me remember Your healing Words in every situation."

Jesus' Words that Point to this Commandment

Matthew 7:21, Matthew 24:14, Matthew 28:19-20, Mark 16:15, Luke 10:27, Luke 11:28, Luke 17:21, John 5:19-20, John 12:49-50, John 15:10

> *Jesus said, "The kingdom is not discovered in one place or another, for God's kingdom realm is already expanding within some of you."*
> *Luke 17:21 TPT*

How can I apply this to my life?

____

____

____

____

____

____

____

____

____

____

Keep this Book of the Law always on your lips; meditate on it day and night, so that you may be careful to do everything written in it. Then you will be prosperous and successful. Joshua 1:8

Accept My Sacrifice.

Red Letters

Peter persisted, "You're not going to wash my feet—ever!"
Jesus said, "If I don't wash you, you can't be part of what I'm doing."
John 13:8 MSG

Peter wanted to be in charge of keeping his own feet clean. He was embarrassed to let his Master and the Anointed Son of God do his dirty-work. How often do we try to make ourselves look good and holy in the sight of God? How often do we try to follow all the rules and fall short? How often do we try to keep ourselves clean from sin and fail?

When He held Peter's feet in His hands, Jesus knew the time had come for His own innocent blood to be shed on the cross as an atonement for our sin. There was no other way to be cleansed except by Him.

1 John 1:7 says, "and the blood of Jesus His Son cleanses us from every sin." God chose the very best He had to cleanse us. He chose the blood of His beloved Son to wash us clean.

There is no other way to be free from the contamination of sin. Without this cleansing, sin will separate us from God, and bring destruction to everything we call our own.

To be Jesus' follower is not the result of Christian works, but it is humbling yourself to let the King of kings wash you clean.

Accept His sacrifice as your own payment. He has paid the price to set you free.

You are washed clean. Now live for Him.

<u>Prayer</u>

"Jesus, You did the work. I couldn't cleanse myself enough, so You cleansed me perfectly. I couldn't die for myself, so You died for me. I couldn't pay a punishment with enough sickness or pain, so You did that for me. Thank you for washing me clean of sin, sickness and death through Your sacrifice."

<u>Jesus' Words that Point to this Commandment</u>

Matthew 26:27-28, Mark 1:41, Mark 14:23-24, Luke 22:20,44, John 13:3-9, John 19:33-34

> *"And when Jesus had taken a cup [of wine] and given thanks, He gave it to them, and they all drank from it. And He said to them, "This is My blood of the [new] covenant, [My blood] which is being poured out for many [for the forgiveness of sins]."*
>
> *Mark 14:23-24 AMP*

How can I apply this to my life?

____

____

____

____

____

____

____

The world and its desires pass away, but whoever does the will of God lives forever. 1 John 2:17

Understand Our Covenant.

Red Letters

Jesus said, "Truly, anyone welcoming My messenger is welcoming Me. And to welcome Me is to welcome the Father who sent Me."
John 13:20 TLB

Covenant is a very serious agreement that is based on a lifelong commitment to support, protect, and stand with the one you are in covenant with, even in the face of death. What belongs to one covenant partner belongs to the other.

God's covenant with the Israelites included the law and He required sacrifice and obedience to that law. The new covenant has Jesus as it's Mediator and it is through His sacrifice and obedience an eternal inheritance is poured out to us from the Father. Our only requirement is to believe in the Son of God, Jesus Christ.

In the scripture above, Jesus is showing us a picture of our new covenant relationship with Him and the Father.
Simply put: 1. God sent His son, Jesus. 2. When you received Jesus, and His sacrifice on the cross, you receive God as your Father. You are now a part of the family of God. 3. Jesus now sends you out to the world, and those who receive you and your testimony, receive Jesus.

Jesus promises, "I am in them and they are in Me" (John 17:23).

Wherever you go, He goes. You are not only adopted, but your inner-man is now made with God's spirit. You are part of His immediate family.

You are a partaker of the eternal covenant between Jesus and the Father. We are all connected with a tie that cannot be broken.

You will never be forsaken. You will never be left alone. The covenant is locked and His power goes with you.

Prayer

"Lord, everything that is important to me, is important to You. Everything that is important to You, is important to me. Today, I acknowledge that I am not alone. Wherever I go, You go also. The greatest One of all is for me and I am not powerless because You live in me."

Jesus' Words that Point to this Commandment

Matthew 10:40, Matthew 28:18-20, Luke 9:48, Luke 22:14-20, John 13:20, John 14:21, John 15:14-19, John 17:10-23, John 20:21

> *Jesus said, "Peace be unto you: as my Father hath sent me, even so send I you." John 20:21 KJV*

How can I apply this to my life?

___

___

___

___

___

___

___

___

___

___

When You are Betrayed, Stay Focused on God.

Red Letters

Follow Me in this:

(Judas left to betray Him.) Jesus said, "The time has come for the glory of God to surround the Son of Man, and God will be greatly glorified through what happens to Me. And very soon God will unveil the glory of the Son of Man." John 13:31-32 TPT

When Judas betrayed Jesus, Jesus had every right to ask him, "Why Judas? What did I do to hurt you?" He had every right to say, "You sold Me out, what were you thinking?"

Jesus didn't confront him, call him names, or condemn him for his choice. He didn't talk to the others about Judas. He released him.

Then Jesus turned His heart to the One who would never betray Him, His Father God. He looked to the authority of His loving Father and the relationship He had with Him. Like placing a protective barrier over His heart, He spoke God's promises concerning His life and peace rose up. He changed His focus from the betrayal to the victory God promised. We are now given salvation because of His obedience.

When someone you trust hurts you, release them. Keep glorifying God. Put your trust in His perfect justice.

When you decide to give God glory, you also are lifted up and out of that situation.

Prayer

"Lord, you know how badly it hurts to be let down by someone You trust. I will not pay attention to this wrong I have suffered. I release them. Heal my heart and lead me to be an overcomer in this situation."

Jesus' Words that Point to this Commandment

Matthew 6:8-15, Luke 23:20-25,34, John 13:31-35, John 17:1

> *While they were nailing Jesus to the cross, He prayed over and over, "Father forgive them, for they don't know what they are doing."*
> *Luke 23:34 TPT*

How can I apply this to my life?

____

____

____

____

____

____

____

____

____

But even though He was a wonderful Son, He learned to listen and obey through all His sufferings. And after being proven in this way He has now become the source of eternal salvation to all those who listen to Him and obey. Hebrews 5:8-9 TPT

Build Up the Kingdom of God on Earth.

Red Letters

"I assure you, most solemnly I tell you, if anyone steadfastly believes in Me, he will himself be able to do the things that I do; and he will do even greater things than these, because I go to the Father." John 14:12 AMP

Jesus laid the foundation for the kingdom of God here on earth, and as believers, we partner with Him to build it up. Staying within the blueprint God designed and following what Jesus has said, we build up His church. It is our job to increase and grow and not to tear down and destroy.

As we build, we focus on the world and their need for Jesus, not on building walls within the body of Christ.

Imagine the beauty of that church if everyone reflected the light of Jesus. Every part of the structure, transparent and brilliant. Different designs and purposes flowing seamlessly together. We would be the light of the world and a city that cannot be hidden.

We are not a broken church. We are the victorious church that reflects the true authority of Christ on the earth. We are a church who knows the ground we stand on. The walls and gates are untouchable by the power of death. We stand in unity, firmly rooted and grounded in love, until He returns.

Building and increasing means doors need to be open, inside and outside. It means the new can be built upon the old. It means the body of Christ is of one mind and purpose.

Abraham dreamed and believed there would one day be this miraculous structure. He travelled throughout the land repeatedly putting up a tent to honor God and all the while he was setting his eyes of faith on a church with "an unshakable foundation, whose architect and builder is God Himself" (Hebrews 11:10).

We are that church.

Prayer

"Lord, give me a heart for unity in the body of Christ, Your church. Show me what I can do to build up Your victorious Kingdom of God here on the earth. Teach me, Lord what you would have me build."

Jesus' Words that Point to this Commandment

Matthew 4:17, Matthew 6:33, Matthew 7:21-23, Matthew 13:18-30, Matthew 16:18, Matthew 28: 16-20, John 4:37, John 14:8-14, John 14:23, John 18:36

Jesus said, "And this rock will be the bedrock foundation on which I will build my church...and the power of death will not be able to overpower it! Matthew 16:18 TPT

How can I apply this to my life?

Receive the Holy Spirit.

Red Letters

Jesus said, "I will ask the Father, and He will give you another advocate to help you and be with you forever-the Spirit of Truth. The world cannot accept Him, because it neither sees Him or knows Him. But you know Him, for He lives with you and will be in you."

John 14:17 NIV

How many times have you thought, "If only Jesus was right here with me now, I would know what to do?" Jesus is on the throne of all authority. He has ascended, and lives in heaven. And...He isn't apart from us.

Jesus never left His followers to fend for themselves on the earth. He knew we would need someone to guide us in the Way, teach us the principles of the Kingdom, remind us of His words, battle the enemy by our side, and comfort us during the storms of life. He has given us the Holy Spirit.

He is the Spirit of Truth. He is the power of Christ. He is your Teacher, your Guide, and your Comforter. He is sent to live with you forever and you will never be alone. This is not a gift for the world but only for the followers of Jesus.

After Jesus had risen from the grave, He came upon His friends who believed in Him and the bible tells us He breathed on them and said, "Receive the Holy Spirit" (John 20:21). Like His friends, do you believe Jesus died for your sins, was buried, and on the third day rose from the grave and is alive today, seated at the right hand of God? If so, then Jesus breathes on you His gift of the Holy Spirit. It comes with a releasing of His peace over your entire being.

There is an even deeper move of the Holy Spirit available to you. It is a soaking or baptism of the Holy Spirit and comes as a result of boldly praying (Acts 4:31). It is the indwelling of the power of the Holy Spirit and it will move you to go into all the world and proclaim what Jesus has done for you. It takes you into a deeper intimacy with Him.
John 14:17 speaks of the Holy Spirit "living with you AND will be in you": two levels of walking with Holy Spirit.

If you have never done this, simply pray and ask, "Jesus baptize me with the Holy Spirit." He will fill you. When He fills you, you will receive a prayer language unlike any language you have heard.

Prayer

"Holy Spirit fill me. I yield to You today. Fill my wounds with healing. Fill my confusion with Your perfect wisdom. Fill my mouth with a language only for You. Help me pray the perfect prayer for my life and those I love."

Jesus' Words that Point to this Commandment

Mark 1:8, Mark 13:11, Luke 4:14, Luke 11:13, Luke 12:12, John 14:16-18, 26, John 16:7, John 20:21-22

> *Jesus said, "And if even sinful persons like yourselves give children what they need, don't you realize that your heavenly Father will do at least as much, and give the Holy Spirit to those who ask for him?"*
> *Luke 11:13 TLB*

How can I apply this to my life?

____

____

____

____

Don't Let the Devil Own Anything in You.

Red Letters

Follow Me in this:

"I don't have much more time to talk to you, for the evil prince of this world approaches. He has no power over me, but I will freely do what the Father requires of me so that the world will know that I love the Father. Come, let's be going." John 14:30 TLB

Jesus said, "The prince of this world has NOTHING in me" (John 14:30 KJV). The devil owned nothing in Jesus.

Check your desires. Are there any heart strings tied to the world?

Jesus loved the Father more than the world...more than Himself. His Father was His only authority. He said, "I only do those things which the Father tells Me." His desire was solely connected with His Father God.

Make it a regular habit to check your heart. Has a desire for power crept in or has a desire for worldly comfort started to dictate your choices? Has a fear of your future begun to take root? Have your eyes wandered to another person's life and do you yearn for what they have?

There are many ways our thoughts can create hooks the enemy can hold onto. When those hooks are established, he can yank on your emotions and then your actions will follow.

Clean house, repent, and renew your mind with the promises of God - submit your entire life to those promises.

If you do this, the devil will have nothing in you.

Prayer

"Lord, the world and its distractions have taken my focus. Forgive me. I will make the decision, today, to set my heart on things that are eternal. I will keep my heart from the influence of the evil one by staying focused on You."

Jesus' Words that Point to this Commandment

Matthew 4:1-11, Matthew 16:23-24, John 8:6, John 12:31, John 14:30-31

Jesus turned on Peter and said, "Get away from me, you Satan! You are a dangerous trap to me. You are thinking merely from a human point of view, and not from God's."

Matthew 16:23 TLB

How can I apply this to my life?

"I have no need to be validated by men, but I'm saying these things so that you will believe and be rescued." - Jesus, John 5:33 TPT

Be Vitally Connected to Me.

Red Letters

"Yes, I am the Vine; you are the branches. Whoever lives in me and I in him shall produce a large crop of fruit. For apart from me you can't do a thing....

If you live in Me [abide vitally united to Me] and My words remain in you and continue to live in your hearts, ask whatever you will, and it shall be done for you."

John 15: 5,7 AMP

If Jesus were to speak to today's audience, He might use an illustration of an astronaut attached by a tether to his ship.

If an astronaut stepped away from the ship without a tether, he would not live. If an astronaut's tether started to fray, pull apart and rip away from the ship, the astronaut would be released into darkness. He would float away into certain death. His resources might last for a while but at some point, he would perish.

That tether is Jesus. He is your vital connection to eternal life.

To believe in Jesus and His finished work at the cross, means you are in Christ. You are connected eternally. He says to you, "As you live in life-union with Me as your source, fruitfulness will stream from within you-but when you live separated from Me you are powerless" (John 15:5 TPT). When you are connected to Jesus you are sustained by living promises which are a source of life-giving water. You are fed with the bread of life. You are nourished with His love.

The fibers of that connection are strengthened by your faith in His promises.

A threefold cord is not easily broken: That cord is Jesus, the Word, and you.
You are connected to Father God when you have life-union with Jesus.

You can ask Him for anything, lined up with the Word of God, and it will be done. As a result, your life will produce something amazing.

Prayer

"Lord, You have planted me in Your kingdom. I am called a child of God. Your Word says I am a 'tree of righteousness planted by the Lord' (Isaiah 61). I am rooted and grounded in Your love. My life-veins are continually filled with Your living water when I read Your Word. This will protect me. Let everything that I produce give You glory!"

Jesus' Words that Point to this Commandment

John 8:31-32, John 9:33, John 10:10, John 13:35, John 15:1-17, Luke 13:2-9

> *Jesus said, "If you keep my commands, you will live in my love, just as I have kept my Father's commands, for I continually live nourished and empowered by His love." John 15:10 TPT*

How can I apply this to my life?

____

____

____

____

____

____

____

____

Do Not Let Your Love for God Grow Cold.

Red Letters

Jesus said, "Many will stop following Me and fall away...There will be such an increase of sin and lawlessness that those whose hearts once burned with passion for God and others will grow cold. But keep your hope to the end and you will experience life and deliverance."

Matthew 24:10-13 TPT

The current that the world creates will try to push against you and send you away from God. Stay focused on Jesus.

Every night cast your cares in prayer.
Every morning declare His promises over your life.
Every hour seek His wisdom and never release the peace of God for the cares of this age.
Go where He tells you. His love will always be there.

Little by little, like water wearing away the earth, the struggles of life will try to pull you away from God. There is a danger you could get carried away and find yourself living by the world's values, and your love for God becoming increasingly colder. Be diligent to never let this happen.

The great day of the Lord is very close.

Prayer

"Lord I turn my heart toward You. Thank you for never taking Your eyes off of me. Thank you for loving me just as I am. I lay down everything at Your throne that has separated me from You."

Jesus' Words that Point to this Commandment

Matthew 24:12-14,42, Matthew 25:1-13, Matthew 26:41, Mark 13:33-37, Mark 14:38, Luke 12:35-40,43-48, Luke 17:26-37, Luke 21:33-36

> *Jesus said, ""But be on guard, so that your hearts are not weighed down and depressed with the giddiness of debauchery and the nausea of self-indulgence and the worldly worries of life, and then that day [when the Messiah returns] will not come on you suddenly like a trap; for it will come upon all those who live on the face of all the earth. But keep alert at all times [be attentive and ready], praying that you may have the strength and ability [to be found worthy and] to escape all these things that are going to take place, and to stand in the presence of the Son of Man [at His coming]." Luke 21:33-36 AMP*

How can I apply this to my life?

____

____

____

____

____

____

____

____

____

"When you obey my heavenly Father, that makes you a part of my true family."- Jesus, Matthew 12:50

Receive My Friendship.

Red Letters

> *Jesus said, "I have never called you 'servants', because a master doesn't confide in His servants, and servants don't always understand what the Master is doing. But I call you My most intimate friends, for I reveal to you everything I have heard from My Father." John 15:15 TPT*

The relationship Jesus desires with you is not a relationship of general and soldier. It is not between high teacher and lowly student. It is not even lord and servant...it is a friendship. Jesus calls YOU friend.

Friendship is defined as "a state of mutual trust and support between allies." He has your back. Your enemies are His enemies and His enemies are yours. He wants you to sit with Him, shoulder to shoulder, and see the world as He sees it. He wants to hear your dreams and have you hear His.

Unlike servanthood, friendships are chosen, then nurtured and developed. They come from intimacy and understanding the passions of someone else. When you become a friend of Jesus you grow a deeper love for the lost in the world. You become a friend to the weak. You desire righteous causes. You also gain a friend who understands what puts a smile on YOUR face.

As it often is with alliances, when the world wants nothing to do with you because you call Him friend, remember, it hated Him first. He will remind you that He has overcome the world.

Every person can be defined by the friends they choose. Choose to receive the friendship of Jesus.

Prayer

"Lord Jesus, my friend. I want to know You more. I want to trust You with all of my heart. I want to hear Your opinion about everything that is on my mind. I want to hear what is on Your mind."

Jesus' Words that Point to this Commandment

Luke 12:4 (addresses you as friend), John 13:34-35, John 15:12-19

> *Jesus said, "No one has greater love [nor stronger commitment] than to lay down his own life for his friends." John 15:13 AMP*

How can I apply this to my life?

One who has unreliable friends soon comes to ruin, but there is a friend who sticks closer than a brother. Proverbs 18:24

Persecution Will Come. Don't Be Afraid.

Red Letters

"I've told you these things to prepare you for rough times ahead. They are going to throw you out of the meeting places. There will even come a time when anyone who kills you will think he's doing God a favor. They will do these things because they never really understood the Father. I've told you these things so that when the time comes, and they start in on you, you'll be well-warned and ready for them." John 16:1-4 MSG

The world's philosophy of "do/get what makes you happy" (at any cost) and Jesus' teachings do not mix.

When you take a stand for Jesus and everything He taught (not just a part of it) persecutions will come. Part of being a friend of Jesus includes persecution.

Be comforted by the fact Jesus told you this would happen if you are a true follower. When you are harassed because you have aligned yourself with Christian principles, Jesus warned you this would happen. When you are treated unfairly in the public systems and governments because you believe in the Bible, Jesus warned you it would happen.
When people accuse you unfairly of not being tolerant but do not tolerate your beliefs, Jesus warned you.

Sadly, religious people (those who follow rules, apart from the words of the bible) may be the ones who persecute you the most. They may push you away. They may speak evil against you. They may try to do worse and they will think they are doing God's will.

Don't be offended or anxious. Keep loving people and follow Jesus.

He has promised to defend your reputation and protect you (Isaiah 54:17).

Prayer

"Lord, fill me with Your holy courage. I am submitted to You, my God. Take any fear of man from my heart. I will honor You and Your Word all the days of my life."

Jesus' Words that Point to this Commandment

Matthew 5:10-12, Matthew 5:44-48, John 12:35-43, John 15:18-27, John 16:1-4

Jesus said, "If you belonged to the world, the world would love [you as] its own and would treat you with affection. But you are not of the world [you no longer belong to it], but I have chosen you out of the world. And because of this the world hates you." John 15:19 AMP

How can I apply this to my life?

____

____

____

____

____

____

____

____

Whether you turn to the right or to the left, your ears will hear a voice behind you saying, "This is the way; walk in it." Isaiah 31:21

Receive God's Love.

Red Letters

> *"The Father Himself loves you dearly because you love me and believe that I came from the Father." John 16:27 TLB*

God loves you. His love does not fluctuate with how good you can be. God's love is the love that you have always longed for; it is a perfect love.

It is impossible to follow Jesus without first receiving His love. Your eternal salvation was birthed and made possible from this love. The only way to truly worship God is to know how deeply He loves you. If you are to love your enemies as Jesus commanded, then you must be first filled with God's love for you.

Wherever you are in your faith walk, stop for a moment, and receive the love of God new and afresh today.
Let His love pour over you.
Let His love cover your mind and every thought you have.
Let His love pour into your heart. "His love is poured into our hearts by the Holy Spirit" (Romans 5:5).

Let His love cleanse every desire in your heart, creating good soil for His promises. Let His love touch every cell in your body, restoring and healing. As it pours through your body to the soles of your feet, let yourself be rooted and grounded in this love.

This is the substance that makes you more than a conqueror in life.
This is the part of you that cannot fail.

Through Jesus' death and resurrection, you have entered into a love that is without end. Your whole being and His love are entwined together and there is nothing you can do to release it.

Prayer

"Lord, I receive Your love today. It is a love that never changes. It overflows to fill me and make me whole. Thank You for Your great love for me."

Jesus' Words that Point to this Commandment

John 3:16-17, John 13:34-35, John 14:23, John 15:13, John 15:16-23, John 16:22-27, John 17:13-23

> *Jesus answered, "If anyone [really] loves Me, he will keep My word (teaching); and My Father will love him, and We will come to him and make Our dwelling place with him." John 14:23 AMP*

How can I apply this to my life?

____

____

____

____

____

____

In all these things we are more than conquerors through Him who loved us. For I am convinced that neither death nor life, neither angels nor demons, neither the present nor the future, nor any powers, neither height nor depth, nor anything else in all creation, will be able to separate us from the love of God that is in Christ Jesus our Lord.

Romans 8:37-39

Get to Work on Your Kingdom Business.

Red Letters

Follow Me in this:

"I have glorified You down here on the earth by completing the work that You gave Me to do." John 17:4 AMP

Your hands, your feet, your mouth, your arms, your time, your heart should be doing the work you have been called to do. There is so much to receive in the Christian life but there is equally so much to give.
The followers of Jesus are called to be leaders.

The world is full of people who are "hungry" for you to take a stand for what you believe and act on it. They want you to be the salt of the earth. They want you to be a light in a dark place. They want you to stand for righteousness. They covet your prayers. They need your hands to help them and they do not want compromise or political correctness.
Take your stand and let the life of God flow out of everything you do.

Go into the world and increase the Kingdom of Heaven one child, one mother, one father, one man, one woman at a time. Win them over with the love God has poured into you.

Teach others about God's life-giving Word, pray for them, and feed "His lambs." Your life's purpose is to glorify God on this earth.

Prayer

"Lord, let Your will be done here on earth as it is in Heaven. I desire a heavenly perspective on my life. I want to focus on things that are eternal and not on those things that will decay with the earth."

Jesus' Words that Point to this Commandment

Matthew 5:16, Matthew 16:18-19, Matthew 28:18-20, John 6:37-40, John 14:12, John 17:1,4-9, John 21:15-17

> *So when they had finished breakfast, Jesus said to Simon Peter, "Simon, son of John, do you love Me more than these [others do—with total commitment and devotion]?" He said to Him, "Yes, Lord; You know that I love You [with a deep, personal affection, as for a close friend]." Jesus said to him, "Feed My lambs." John 21:15 AMP*

How can I apply this to my life?

____

____

____

____

____

____

____

____

____

We have become His poetry, a re-created people that will fulfill the destiny He has given each of us, for we are joined to Jesus, the Anointed One. Even before we were born, God planned in advance our destiny and the good works we would do to fulfill it!

Ephesians 1:10 TPT

Let Your Life Reveal the Truth With, or Without, Words.

Red Letters

Follow Me in this:

"And blessed (happy, fortunate, and to be envied) is he who takes no offense at Me and finds no cause for stumbling in or through Me and is not hindered from seeing the Truth."

Matthew 11:6 AMP

When the Roman ruler, Pilate, asked Jesus, "What is truth?" (John 18:38) Jesus was silent.

When you walk with the Lord and follow His commandments your life will hold a fragrance of Truth. Your actions will testify of God's love in your life. Some will be drawn toward it, and some will be repelled.

Jesus was aware that Pilate was repelled by it and so He kept silent. He let His actions speak instead of wasting His words on hard ground.

Always seek the mind of the Lord. Bear witness in your life of God's Truth and you will be heard by those that CAN hear the truth. Don't try to make those who can't hear the Truth hear it. Like hard ground, they don't want it.

Jesus said, "I am the Way, the Truth and the Life. No one comes to the Father except through Me" (John 14:6). When you follow Jesus and reflect Him in your life, His Truth will be evident.

Prayer

"Lord, guide me in Your Truth. Help me to live in Your Truth in every

area of my life today. Help me to not be conformed to this world but transformed by Your powerful Truth."

Jesus' Words that Point to this Commandment

Matthew 11:6-15,25-30, Matthew 13:15-16, Mark 4:21-25, John 1:17, John 4: 24, John 8:31-32, John 17:17, John 18:37-38, John 19:7-9

> *So Pilate said to Him, "Then You are a King?" Jesus answered, "You say [correctly] that I am a King. This is why I was born, and for this I have come into the world, to testify to the truth. Everyone who is of the truth [who is a friend of the truth and belongs to the truth] hears and listens carefully to My voice." Pilate said to Him [scornfully], "What is truth?" John 18:37-38 AMP*

How can I apply this to my life?

Do your best to present yourself to God as one approved, a worker who does not need to be ashamed and who correctly handles the Word of Truth. 2 Timothy 2:15

Guard Your Thought Life.

Red Letters

> *Jesus said, "Your souls aren't harmed by what you eat, but by what you think and say!"*
> *Mark 7:15 TLB*

The mind is a gift from God and it is your own. Because of free will, you alone are the ruler of your thoughts.

Evil thoughts and good thoughts circle your mind every day like birds who circle a nest. You choose what thoughts make their home in your mind. Proverbs 23:7 says, "As a man thinks...so is he."

Our countenance reflects our thoughts. Our words reflect our thoughts. Our actions are all a reflection of our thoughts.

The religious men, then and now, look to the actions of men and try to correct them. Jesus said it is the thoughts of a man that pollute him.

How do you control your thoughts? You catch them. Awareness is key. Ask yourself, "Is that thought true?" Cast down the ones that are not.

The Holy Spirit reminds us that we have help in the Word: "The Word of God is quick and powerful...it is a discerner of the thoughts and intents of the heart" (Hebrews 4:12). The scriptures help you discern what is evil, so that you can take the negative thought captive and cast it down as a lie.

For example, a fearful thought may come to you regarding death.
Grab that thought and speak to it. Thoughts do not overcome thoughts. What you speak overcomes a thought.

You might say, "I will not die. I will live because Jesus said in John 10:10 that He came that I may have life and have it abundantly."

You have placed life in your thoughts, on your tongue, and in your entire being. Taking captive every thought to make it obedient to Christ (2 Corinthians 10:5) will set your course toward an abundant life.

Prayer

"Lord, anoint my mind. I have the mind of Christ. I take control of every evil thought and cast it out of my mind. Help me to think on those things that are good and perfect. Wash my mind with your living Word."

Jesus' Words that Point to this Commandment

Matthew 5:27-28, Matthew 12:43-45, Matthew 15:8-11, Mark 7:20-23

> *And then Jesus added, "It is the thought-life that pollutes. For from within, out of men's hearts, come evil thoughts of lust, theft, murder, adultery, wanting what belongs to others, wickedness, deceit, lewdness, envy, slander, pride, and all other folly. All these vile things come from within; they are what pollute you and make you unfit for God."*
>
> *Mark 7:20-23 TLB*

How can I apply this to my life?

Know My Voice.

Red Letters

(After Jesus' resurrection) Jesus spoke to them: "Good morning! Did you catch anything for breakfast?" They answered, "No." He said, "Throw the net off the right side of the boat and see what happens." They did what he said. All of a sudden there were so many fish in it, they weren't strong enough to pull it in.

Then the disciple Jesus loved said, "It's the Master!"

John 21:5-7 MSG

Know the voice of Jesus.

John had a personal relationship with Jesus. He recognized His voice. Jesus had resurrected from the dead in the above scripture and was not recognizable. But John *knew* his Savior's voice. At the last supper, John had his head leaning toward Jesus' heart (John 13:23-25). He kept his ear close to his Savior's voice.

You need to recognize Jesus' voice.
You will hear it in the gospels as He speaks through the red letters.
You will hear His voice in every scripture from the beginning to the end.
You will hear it in your heart quietly directing your steps.

You will need to know His voice as the times get darker. It will be critical you hear Him.

Jesus will help you with what you need, if you trust in Him. Make it a habit to consult Him concerning everything. You will hear His direction. It comes with peace.

He came to partner with you in your life. This is not called religion. This is relationship.

Prayer

"Lord, I hear Your voice and I will not listen to the enemy. I will regularly be still and listen with my heart. Thank you for Your voice. Make my path plain and guide me."

Jesus' Words that Point to this Commandment

John 10:1-5,15-16, John 10:27, John 15:15-16, John 16:13-15, John 21:1-12

Jesus said, "The sheep that are My own hear My voice and listen to Me; I know them, and they follow Me." John 10:27 AMP

How can I apply this to my life?

____

____

____

____

____

____

____

____

____

"It is the Spirit who gives life; the flesh is no help at all. The words that I have spoken to you are spirit and life."-Jesus, John 6:63

It is Time. Turn from Sin and Turn to God.

Red Letters

Jesus summed it all up when he cried out, "Whoever believes in me, believes not just in me but in the One who sent me. Whoever looks at me is looking, in fact, at the One who sent me. I am Light that has come into the world so that all who believe in me won't have to stay any longer in the dark." John 12:44 MSG

The first sin in the garden of Eden was put into motion by human reasoning or understanding. You could say Adam and Eve thought, "I know what God says, but it's my life, I think the serpent is right. I will know better, and I *need* this." Their eyes turned to themselves in that moment, then they turned to the fruit (Genesis 3:2-6). Their connection to God was broken. They turned their back on God and faced their sin.

Repentance means to turn your back on the sin and turn to God.
When we make the choice to repent and turn away from the sin, and not make excuses for it, we allow God to heal us.

Jesus tells us to look at Him. No matter where you are - even if you are drowning in sin - as you look in the face of God, He embraces you like the father of the prodigal son (Luke 15:11-32). He pulls you toward Him and He crowns you with loving-kindness and mercy. He calls you His child. Embraced by the Light of the Father, you are now a child of the Light.

Don't put one foot in the world and one foot in God's kingdom. You do not have all the time in the world to go back and forth.
It is time to repent. The Kingdom of God is at hand.
Be all in.

It is impossible to be in the light and in darkness at the same time.

Prayer

"Forgive me, Lord. I take responsibility and turn from my sin and turn to You. I look into Your loving eyes and reveal my heart to You. I receive Your embrace."

Jesus' Words that Point to this Commandment

Matthew 4:12-17, Matthew 21:28-32, Mark 1:14-15, Luke 5:31-32, John 6:29, John 6:35-40, John 12: 46

From that time Jesus began to preach and say, "Repent [change your inner self—your old way of thinking, regret past sins, live your life in a way that proves repentance; seek God's purpose for your life], for the kingdom of heaven is at hand." Matthew 4:17 AMP

How can I apply this to my life?

Teach the Nations About Me.

Red Letters

Then Jesus came close to them and said, "All the authority of the universe has been given to Me. Now wherever you go, make disciples of all nations, baptizing them in the name of the Father, the Son, and the Holy Spirit. And teach them to faithfully follow all that I have commanded you." Mathew 28:18-20 TPT

When Jesus spoke this commandment, He had just risen from the dead, defeating sin and death for us all. He had just been given ALL power in Heaven and Earth.

This is the first message God gave the risen Jesus to deliver to us: "Teach the nations about Me and baptize them in the name of the Father and of the Son and the Holy Spirit. Teach them My commandments and remember I am with you always."

He is giving us marching orders to go and spread the Good News. All of us. Not just a select few. It is significant because through Jesus' resurrection, we are now ONE with Him. We don't just go with a good message. We go with a solid promise that Jesus has overcome the world for us. (Revelation 12:10-11)

We are now part of a family of over-comers. Sin and its destruction have been overcome. Don't keep that exciting reality a secret. Share it. Go tell the world He has overcome and in Him, so have we!

Prayer

"Lord, use me. You have given me special talents and abilities for the purpose of spreading Your gospel. When I use these talents on myself,

for my glory, life is empty. When I use them for Your glory I am filled with real life!"

Jesus' Words that Point to this Commandment

Matthew 10:7-14, 32, Matthew 28:18-20, Mark 1:15, Mark 5:19-20, Mark 16:15-18, Luke 9:1-6, Luke 9:60-62, Luke 10:2-16, Luke 10:17-20, Luke 24:44-49, John 3:16-17, John 17:6-26

> *Jesus said, "As you go into all the world, preach openly the wonderful news of the gospel to the entire human race! Whoever believes the good news and is baptized will be saved, and whoever does not believe the good news will be condemned. And these miracle signs will accompany those who believe: They will drive out demons in the power of My name. They will speak in tongues. They will be supernaturally protected by snakes and from drinking anything poisonous. And they will lay hands on the sick and heal them." Mark 16:15-18 MSG*

How can I apply this to my life?

Pray This Way.

Red Letters

Jesus said, "When you pray, don't babble on and on as the Gentiles do. They think their prayers are answered merely by repeating their words again and again. Don't be like them, for your Father knows exactly what you need even before you ask him!

Pray like this:

Our Father in heaven, may your name be kept holy.

May your Kingdom come soon. May your will be done on earth, as it is in heaven. Give us today the food we need, and forgive us our sins, as we have forgiven those who sin against us. And don't let us yield to temptation but rescue us from the evil one. Amen." Matthew 6:7-13 NLT

1. *ADDRESS*

"Our Father, Who art in Heaven." Matthew 6:9

Begin by boldly entering into prayer acknowledging God as your Father. This is the first time in <u>all</u> the scriptures God is addressed as Heavenly Father. Through Jesus, we enter into this close relationship and accept our identity as a child of God.

"Father, You know everything that concerns me. I am Your child. You are my Father because of the precious blood of Jesus."

2. *HONOR*

"Holy is Your Name." Matthew 6:9

The Name of the Lord is holy. It is a place where you can enter in and be safely surrounded. Proverbs 18:10 tells us that "The name of the Lord is a strong tower and the righteous run into it and they are safe". There is no name that is above His name! There is no safer refuge than in His holy name.

"Bless Your holy name! You are the Lord my Healer (Jehovah-rophe). The Lord my Righteousness (Jehovah-tsidkenu). The Lord my Peace (Jehovah-shalom). The Lord who never leaves me (Jehovah-shammah). You are the Lord my Shepherd (Jehovah-rohi). You are the Lord who provides for me (Jehovah-jireh). You are the Lord that cleanses me (Jehovah-m'kaddesh). You place Your Holy Name like a banner above me."

3. *DECLARE*

"Your kingdom will come and Your will {your word} will be done on earth as it is in heaven." Matthew 6:10

Jesus said, "If someone says to this mountain with great faith and having no doubt, 'Mountain be lifted up and thrown into the sea' and believes that what he says will happen, it will be done. This is the reason I urge you to boldly believe for whatever you ask for in prayer-be convinced you have received it and it will be yours." (Mark 11:23-24 TPT). Declare the rich blessings of His promises over your life and others. His Word *is* His promise and God always keeps His promises.
"I pray Your Kingdom would be here on earth like it is in Heaven. Help me build Your Kingdom. I pray Your will for my life to come to pass. I pray Your goodness and mercy over my household, my church, and my nation. I declare Your healing on earth as it is in heaven."

4. *ASK*

"Give us today our daily bread." Matthew 6:11

Boldly request your needs. Jesus instructs us that "If you, imperfect as you are, know how to lovingly take care of your children and give them what's best, how much more ready is your heavenly Father to give wonderful gifts to <u>*those who ask Him*</u>" (Matthew 7:11 TPT). The Holy Spirit is in you, reminding you that you are God's beloved child. You no longer need to plead and bargain. Jesus simply says, "Ask".

"I come boldly to Your wonderful throne of grace, Lord and ask that you meet this need. I believe You set a table for me in the presence of my enemies and my cup always overflows. I believe You meet all of my needs, Father, through Your riches and Your glory in Christ, my Savior."

5. *REPENT*

"Forgive us our sins." Matthew 6:12

God commands us all to repent and turn to Him (Acts 17:30). Sin separates us from Him, repentance removes the separation.
Sins are heavy and they constantly condemn us.
Enter into prayer with your Heavenly Father, ask for forgiveness, and believe what is written in 1 John 1:9, "If we confess our sins, He is faithful and just to forgive our sins, and to cleanse us from all unrighteousness".
It is released when you let it go.
"Forgive me for missing the mark. Forgive me for my sins. Forgive me for hurting others and hurting You. There is nothing I am holding back. I repent of my sin."

6. *FORGIVE*

"...as we forgive those who have sinned against us." Matthew 6:12

Forgive others.
You have received God's forgiveness, now release your forgiveness toward others. Jesus tells us we must, or it will hinder our prayers. God's perfect love is poured into you by the Holy Spirit (Romans 5:5), and that love drives out all fear (I John 4:18); Even the fear of forgiving someone who does not deserve it. His love is poured into you until you are filled with the fullness of God (Ephesians 3:18). You are able to forgive, and by doing so you release perfect justice into the Fathers hands.

"I forgive and release all bitterness toward those who have hurt me. I release the need to injure them back. I release them to You."

7. *DELIVERANCE*

"Lead us not into temptation but deliver us from evil." Matthew 6:13

Pray for wisdom and protection. Declare promises of protection over your life. There is an enemy of Jesus and all who are in Christ. He is the accuser of the family of God and a great deceiver. We need, as 1 Peter 5:10 instructs us, to be well balanced and alert. We need to take a stand against the devil and resist every attack with strong vigorous faith. We need to be aware when temptation is near.
"Today, I put on the armor of God. I declare the power of Jesus' sacrifice over my life-the power of His blood. No weapon formed against me is allowed to prosper. The angel of the Lord encamps around me for protection. I walk in the wisdom of God and I hear Your direction, Lord."

8. *PRAISE*

"Yours is the kingdom, the power and the Glory forever!" Matthew 6:13

Release all your power to the One who has all authority and praise Him, for He is without equal! No problem, no sickness, no situation, no difficulty is more powerful than Him. Praise brings the atmosphere of Heaven to earth, right where you stand, praying.
"You reign in Heaven and on the earth. You are my Everlasting Help. You are the author and the finisher of my faith. You are well able! With You nothing is impossible!"

Jesus' Words that Point to this Commandment

Matthew 6:9-13, Luke 11:2-4

React to Sickness in This Way.

Red Letters

Follow Me in this:

While he was still talking to her, messengers arrived from Jairus's home with the news that it was too late—his daughter was dead and there was no point in Jesus' coming now. But Jesus ignored their comments and said to Jairus, "Don't be afraid. Just trust me." Mark 5:35-36 TLB

Jesus never left a man or woman ill who asked (believing) for His healing. Jesus always glorified His Father. God was not glorified in the sickness, God was glorified in the miracle. When you receive a bad health report Jesus teaches us to react to sickness this way:

1. "Don't be afraid. Just trust me." (Mark 5:36)

Speak to the fear and respond to a bad report with your own words. Say aloud, *"I will not be afraid. I believe God loves me. I trust You with all my heart, Lord."*

2. "This sickness is not going to end in death." (John 11:4)

Speak to the sickness, with faith, and take authority over it. Never agree with its power to take your life. *"This sickness does not have more authority over my body than Jesus Christ. Jesus is Lord over my life and He has promised me abundant life."*

3. "God will be glorified." (John 11:4, Mark 5:39)

Speak out the desired result.

"You have given me life, Yahweh. I have given You my life. Use my life as a testimony of how much You love me. Be glorified with my story of healing."

4. "He is asleep and I will awaken him...Your brother will rise again."

It is ok to be real with what you feel and acknowledge the situation, but God's ability to heal is a powerful reality in the kingdom of God. The kingdom of God on the earth is within you (Luke 17:21). Yield to that reality and make it "heavier" than what you see, hear, and feel.

5. Jesus said, "I am the resurrection and the life." (John 11:25)

Keep yourself built up and filled with the Word of God. Remind yourself who Jesus is and who you are in Him. He is your Healer and you are the healed.

6. "Father, I thank you that You have heard me." (John 11:41)

When you are in a battle for your health, it can feel like being in a storm at sea. Doctors, loved ones, even your own mind and body speak from every direction. Up one minute, down the next. Direct your complete focus on God. He is listening. He is your Rock. He is your Peace. He is your Healer. Be filled with faith and be filled with thanksgiving.

7. "When she heard of Jesus, came in the press behind, and touched His garment. For she said, 'If I may touch but His clothes. I shall be whole.' And she was...healed of that plague." (Mark 5:27-29)

Like this woman who heard the report that Jesus was the promised Messiah, her Healer, be strong in faith. Your body may feel weak, like hers, but your inner man can be supernaturally strong. Your inner man becomes strong by feeding your faith with the Word and with prayer. Build up your faith to the point of strong belief, then reach out and receive your miracle.

Jesus' Words that Point to this Commandment

Matthew 9:35, John 11:1-44, Mark 5:21-42

Jesus' Commandments for the Final Days:

1. My Believers will be betrayed by friends and family and brought before worldly rulers to defend their faith. Do not be afraid.

2. When you prepare to defend your faith, do not meditate on the way you will answer. God will give you wisdom and your enemies will not be able to resist the Truth that will be released from your lips.

3. You will be hated because of My name. But know that even death will not harm you.

4. During the chaos of these times, be patient. Be in control of your mind, will, and emotions. Stay humble and gentle. Let My peace be a guard over your heart and mind at all times.

5. There will be false christs and false ideologies. Do not follow them. Diligently spend time in My Word. It will give you the ability to hear My voice, clearly. It will be a matter of life and death to hear My voice.

6. There will be great wars. Do not be afraid.

7. There will be great earthquakes and fearful sights. Do not be afraid.

8. There will be diseases that make people afraid. Keep your eyes on Me.

9. There will be a lack of food in many places. I will meet your need.

10. There will be great signs in the heavens. There will be signs in the sun, the moon, and the stars. Be aware.
What seemed unshakable in the earth's atmosphere will be shaken.

11. Jerusalem will be surrounded by armies and there will be great distress in the land. Jerusalem will be taken over. Do not despair.

12. There will be confusion and fear in all the nations. Men's hearts will stop from fear. Everything man has trusted in, apart from Me, will fail them. Your trust is in Me, do not be afraid.

13. The sea and its great waves will cause global fear.

14. NOW, WHEN YOU SEE AND HEAR THESE THINGS, LOOK UP!
Lift your head, your redemption is near.
You will not miss seeing Me; I will be coming in a cloud with power and great glory.

Jesus' Words that Point to These Commandments

Matthew 24:4-31, Mark 13:5-27, Luke 21:8-28, John 15:18-23

> *"And then—then!—they'll see the Son of Man welcomed in grand style—a glorious welcome! When all this starts to happen, up on your feet. Stand tall with your heads high. Help is on the way!" Luke 21:27-28 MSG*

Meanwhile, the saints stand passionately patient, keeping God's commands, staying faithful to Jesus...God blesses them all for it in the end. Revelation 14:12,13 MSG

Index

Bible Translations

Scripture quotations marked NIV are taken from the Holy Bible, New International Version, NIV. Copyright 1973, 1978, 1984 by Biblica, Inc.
Scripture quotations marked KJV are taken from the King James Version of the Bible.
Scripture quotations marked ESV are taken from the Holy Bible, English Standard Version, copyright 2001 by Crossway Bibles, a division of Good News Publishers.
Scripture quotations marked AMP are taken from the Amplified Bible Copyright 1954, 1958, 1962, 1964, 1965, 1987 by The Lockman Foundation.
Scripture quotations marked MSG are taken from The Message. Copyright 1993, 1994, 1995, 1996, 2000, 2001, 2002.
Scripture quotations marked NKJV are taken from the New King James Version. Copyright 1982, by Thomas Nelson, Inc.
Scripture quotations marked TLB are taken from The Living Bible. Copyright 1971 by Tyndale House Foundation.

Scripture quotations marked TPT are taken from The Passion Translation Bible. Copyright 2017,2018 by Passion and Fire Ministries, Inc.

<u>About the Author</u>

Teresa L. Hoffman is the founder of Holy Ground Life, a unique ministry that centers on entering into the Presence of God. In Exodus 3:5 God tells Moses, "Take off your sandals...for the place you are standing is Holy Ground." She leads others to take off their "sandals" and surrender anything that is separating them from the love of God: stress, sin, worries, burdens, grief, and pain. Through Jesus Christ, Holy Ground is a place of redemption, healing, and restoration. It is a ministry that addresses the whole person: spirit, soul, and body.

Visit holygroundlife.com for more information.

This book was printed because of a generous donation by a follower of Jesus Christ. If you would like to be a part of getting this message out to the world or if you have a church or ministry that would like to receive free copies of this book for new believers, please visit holygroundlife.com and message us.

We believe that it is time to make sure the whole world hears from Jesus.